The World in Our Hands

Adam M. Yeoman

CONTENTS

Economic & Political Lessons From the Past

$\mathcal{T}$he history of our world is marked by many great societies each with their own cultural ideas and values. We, the United States of America are a very young nation among the world. Our history dates back to the initial discovery of the new world starting with attempts by the Vikings and then later exploration and colonization with Columbus and other migrating Europeans who founded Jamestown and St Augustine. Our nation arises out of the population explosion in Europe after the Black Death which decimated Europe's population in the 1300's and lasting until well into the 1500's. This population boom overwhelmed Europe and led to the idea of escaping to a new world. This prompted the immigration to the New World and the buildup of a new nation in an a environment previously held by natives; natives of which were thought to have colonized the new world migrating from Siberia across the Bering Strait to the New World and lived for some 9000 years before coming into contact with Europeans. These early colonizers of the New World have been found by geneticists to come from an Asian heritage along the coast of China.

This is the historical foundation of the United States of America. We are this expansion out of Europe and a branch of European thought and ideology implanted onto a new landscape. As our political and economic systems are a branch off of Europe's tree, we as a society can then trace back our roots to a much earlier time period in Europe to see the evolution of the ideas and imbedded culture among us. The climate in Europe we evolved out of was that of different states and monarchies that can trace their history back almost a thousand years. The country's economic and political systems actually very closely resemble ours. The only difference being is that presidents who are elected and also officials replace Monarchies who are noble from birth and appointed basically government and church officials. The system of hierarchy in society originated from the western society of the last 2000 or so years. This hierarchy in politics and government also became prevalent in economics where social classes develop. This triangular setup of economics predates our industrial boom and capitalism. The thought pattern arose from the separation of the peasant class and the ruling aristocracy. One either was born into aristocracy or appointed into it after success in warfare. This was especially important in English society and is still an important facet even today in Britain with the obsession of the marriage of the royals.

The important lesson from this history of division in social class is that we as westerners are presupposed to having a divided class system with privileged aristocracy. This is in a time where capitalism did not exist in its' current state and we still exhibit the exploitation of the masses for the aristocracy. We can see how certain trends proliferate across time by looking more in depth at the specific historical events in history and especially western history where certain societal trends lead to near collapse for many countries and civilizations.

In Europe many ideas and values in terms of Politics and Economics were being spread by manifestos made by individual philosophers who philosophized on the ideal organization of society in terms of Man's natural state and a society predisposed to cater to this state. Each of these philosophers had been influenced by earlier writers whom wrote in the Roman era, or even pre Roman. Two of the main Roman era philosophers who wrote on Politics and Economics were Plato and Socrates. Plato imagined a Utopian society that is based on justice in every way possible. He actually imagined a version of modern society where each man had a specialty as far as economics is concerned and trade among each-other would occur and all needs would be fulfilled. This however, based on reasonable fair trade and equality. He envisioned people in power to be completely free from parts of the soul that may skew the view of the whole of society.

Socrates envisioned, also a world where reason could stem problems and ills.

This ability for humans to reason and to trust the ability of humans to handle situations correctly with correct reasoning was paramount to his theory. The important aspect of this theory is that in Socrates' time men were subjects of the ruling class and it was widely accepted that peasants could not decide their own fate and that the ruling class must make proper decisions for them. With Aristotle's theory brought the idea of man governing himself using reason as a way to keep proper actions. With Plato's theory came the idea of the perfect organization of society and the search for justice among man's organizations here on Earth. These were the originating ideas of the enlightenment period in Europe. This era was marked by some of the greatest Artists and Scientists in the history of the world for their time. Humans began to use reason and societal organization to achieve things previously unachieved by man. This shift in thought came after the decimation of the black plague in which humans reconsidered their entire world view. This seems to happen after immense disasters. It affects the entire psyche of humanity. Humans before this era were imbedded in the dark ages in which Church aristocracies ruled men and religious purges resulted in genocide of the cruelest fashion. After the mass death that was somewhat a result of the world view of the time, a shift in the human mindset like I said occurred and humans were more focused on what is happening here on earth rather than whichever afterlife they felt awaited for them. The reason for the immense casualties from the Black Death plague was that the focus was more so on religion and prayer rather than figuring out ways of stopping the spread of the disease. People let their garbage pile up and any form of sanitation was halted. This added to huge deaths from the plague and nations such as Italy with very crowded cities experienced horrifying death rates from the plague. This humanism that developed brought the world out of the dark ages and turned focus to creating living conditions on earth instead of focusing completely on the prospects of an afterlife.

This shift was so influential on outcomes in the world because it turned great minds towards all studies of humanity in which were focused on improving the state of the physical world here on earth. This led to the rediscovery of philosophy and traditions that permeated in one of the high periods of human history. This is in order to help form a better future here on Earth. There was a reconsideration of great philosophers such as Plato and Socrates along with other great works. In addition, other forms of knowledge related to architecture and economic production were used to help build Europe out of the Dark Ages. The Renaissance era followed and an enlightened period in Europe started with scientific and humanist revolutions which gave people a great deal more of hope. The idea that we could create almost heavenly conditions on Earth motivated people from everywhere to create a better life. For some, however a different view would proliferate that would lead to suffering, conquest and war for some. The humanist idea also gave greedy and powerful men the idea that they would not be punished for their actions on earth and could simply take a good life from whomever they please. In Italy, Nicolas Machiavelli was exiled from his position on a city court and wrote a manifesto while in exile about man's selfish nature and how in order to attain happiness on Earth you have to control men through power and force. Two competing ideologies came from this. You have the routes of modern capitalist society with Machiavelli and with the Renaissance thought of creating a perfect world ideas of Socialism and modernism developed.

II.

Now you start to see the century's long debate we have had in politics all over the world. Some men and societies believe men to be naturally selfish and in search of power. To create a perfect society to these people is to create a world in which selfishness is rewarded when put into a good cause. Case and point with Adam Smith and his critique of capitalism where selfishness creates progress and there is a trickledown effect to the rest of humanity. Many philosophers wrote manifestos concerning this opinion. Like I mentioned Nicolas Machiavelli and others such as Thomas Hobbes contributed to the theory that humans are bad and need to be controlled to create peace and prosperity. They believe man will only behave rationally if he is forced to. This led in certain areas of Europe to strict dictatorships and societal structures that forced mass laborers working for the benefit of aristocratic classes. This is the thought pattern that created mass industrialism with strict management techniques that launched parts of Europe into the modern industrial era. Counter this thought pattern, which arose out of the elite class as a response to humanism, was the ideas of perfection and justice in society which came from philosophers such as Plato and modern minds such as Karl Marx, Jean Jacque Rousseau and many others. Looking at the foundations of American culture originating in Europe you can use these two concepts to see through a lens of understanding on historical events that occurred as a confliction between these two ideals.

The Renaissance brought the world of the Dark Ages but as I said at the elite level the concept of humanism resulted in power grabbing and control as a way of improving life specifically for the elite. Meanwhile among the people thoughts of justice and fairness among all levels of society permeated. Many of the major European events can be categorized by the competing ideologies of selfishness and control from elite and the equality and justice sought by the masses. Like I said the elite filled a power vacuum that was previously held by the Church in the Dark Ages. It is a very modern concept and still exists today as the wealthy and controllers of industry seek power and control on every level of society. At the time, however there was a social conscious among the people that led to uprisings. In fact, the French Revolution became one of the bloodiest uprisings by the public in European history. This was a direct confliction between the ideas of social justice among society and the rite of the elite to pursue wealth and power on earth. The aristocratic class monopolized money and power

in France and drove it's people to revolt in a
violent fashion in which most of the
aristocracy was killed in public in mass
protest. The anarchy that followed, however,
led to the rise of a military dictator who
tried to seize Europe under Napoleon. At this
same exact period in history, America was
attempting to secede from Britain, and led to
a two front War for England in which they
eventually were driven out of the New World
leading to the proliferation of the United
States of America. Once the world stabilized
after these events modern industrialism was at
the front of events and focus in world affairs
in the western world.

The industrial boom came off a branch of
humanism where people wanted to create the
ideal conditions while living on earth. This
led to a rise in scientific and technological
discoveries which create faster and more
efficient ways of creating all kinds of goods
for humanity. This started early on in Europe
in around the 16th century and became very
prominent in the 17th century and on in the
New World and in Europe. On one hand you have
the embracing of ideas from the Enlightenment
and Renaissance of creating a better physical
world for humans, and on the other you have
people who use it as an excuse to exploit self
interest out of the new industrial era. Again,
this clash led to a rise of new philosophers
debating mans relation to work and
industrialism. On one hand we are shaping our
reality and creating better living conditions
through work, but on the other hand mass
factories and production lines seem to
dehumanize people and lead to exploitation in
the work place and on mass societal levels.

Philosophers such as Jean Jacque Rousseau,
Karl Marx and Immanuel Kant would write
manifestos concerning the relation of man and
this new industrial complex among the world.
Others wrote answers to these texts and used
the idea that selfishness and perceived
exploitation only leads to greater progress.
This is usually the voice of those who own and
control modes of production that attain mass
sums of wealth from mass laborers. To them,
the more work ethic and almost a military
dynamic there is in the work place the more
efficient workers will produce and lead to
even more wealth on their behalf. The major
philosophical concerns raised by authors such
as Karl Marx and Rousseau involve how
industrialism can turn humans into simply
numbers that are only valued for their labor.
The bourgeois class according to Marx will not
stop the exploitation of the masses as they
are not involved in the actual labor. They
simply benefit solely on owning and
controlling production and workers. Marx's
theory calls for a final phase in a cycle of
exploitation where workers and will rise up
against the bourgeois class and create a
democracy and equal sharing of profits under
industrialism.

In many ways the conflict between elite
classes that own and control production and
the masses wishes have been the underwritten
story in thousands of events in the last 400
years. The constant push-pull struggle between
these groups in politics, economics and
general public perception have dominated
discourse among many nations of the world.
This is not just economic exploitation that
has contributed to the uprisings but other

forms as well committed by ruling classes. This, has also been addressed by many philosophers the idea that any ruling class who can drive their ideas and values on the masses is trying to condition society to conform to their views, and if the society feels oppressed it will build and lead to conflict also. Again, through most of history up into the industrial revolution power grabbing and control was instituted by political and church entities. Once the industrial revolution occurred power began to shift into those who could control the products and commodities needed for our civilization.

III.

Selfishness and exploitation previously displayed by political entities are now transitioned into industry where they can exploit mass wealth and intern power in the world. Revolutions that have occurred from this idea are the French Revolution, Russian Revolution, Haitian slave rebellions. There were also countless other events were in some way shaped by the struggle between the controllers and the exploited. In America we have a strong history of workers strikes and long debated movements to create laws that will help stem exploitation from business and create better working conditions for man. Early on in these movements the controlling class attributed any attempt to regulate business labor practices were unsuccessful as courts would point to the 14th amendment of the constitution and attribute corporate regulation to limiting freedoms of the corporations which were considered individuals in the courts eyes. These rulings then led to more protesting by farmers and laborers who were being sold out by the elite classes in America.

In the early 20th century unions became more prominent and forced corporations to behave somewhat fairly to workers. They rose up as a result of events like the coal mining strike crisis in which while on strike the workers shut down coal production and transportation. This led to the president at the time, Theodore Roosevelt, to make concessions to the coal workers and gave hope to those who would bargain for a fair life under capitalism. One of the largest unions that started with around 30 members arose in 1905. The Industrial Workers of the World created hope for unskilled workers around the United States and the world to bargain for a worthwhile life under industrialism. At its' peak it had upwards of 200,000 members. One of the most prominent strikes organized was among 20,000 textile workers. In a time of factory work and dehumanization the union gave pride and hope to these workers. Unfortunately men in power used the fear and dismay of World War One to turn against the Union's and kill and imprison many of them and listing them as foreign agitators. The government would not allow workers to be paid fairly when they needed to build thousands of weapons to try to be the hero in Europe. They used the fear and terror of world war one to create a rally around the flag movement which made anyone who stood in the way of the war effort at traitor. All levels of production were involved in the war effort from textile workers for uniforms to steel workers for weapons. After World War One people who were in power, (i.e. the control group) drove industry with low pay for mass workers and turned record profits never seen before in any industrial country. After World War One leading up to the Great Depression for around 10 years companies used top-down power structures to create compliance among employees and, like I said, it became the roaring twenties with aristocratic classes' experienced immense wealth and luxury. Upper class business owners experienced such boom in profits and luxuries and they then offered products and services to consumers as credit which allowed people to purchase various consumer goods without having the money upfront. This did two things, it contributed profits to the aristocratic class by getting payments that included interest or free money and it also allowed poorer classes to be content with the meager pay that was earned after unions were dismantled. The flow of credit among poor classes created the illusion that they had the life they would have had if they had been paid a fair wage. The only problem with this is that when corporation and aristocratic classes gave credit to the poor classes they never actually took the hit on profits as it was a result of the banking system being able to loan money to corporations, and in turn they could afford to lend money to the poor. This scheme worked for some time as long as consumers could afford the payments and the corporations could refund the banks. The system crashed under itself when consumers experienced decreases in income because of the never ending effort for aristocratic classes to experience more and more luxury while creating less profit for the individual worker. The stock market crash was a result of consumers not being able to pay

their credit bills which in turn the
corporations could not pay the banks and the
banks could not issue any more credit to
corporations. This circular effect bankrupted
the banks and the credit system and therefore
led to the layoff of employees and resulted in
the Great Depression.

IV.

During the Great Depression, much like
today, businesses tightened their belts and
operated at the lowest possible operating
costs as a measure to safeguard against
closure during the recession. Every business,
however, doing this exact thing was partly a
reason for the prolonging of the Depression.
When the movements of jobs, goods and services
slow, consumers start only spending on what is
absolutely necessary and money begins to stop
circulating around businesses leading to
further shrinking of the National economy. We
also implemented protectionist economic
policies which stopped trade with foreign
countries. This also contributed to the
prolonging of the Depression. Franklin
Roosevelt was elected president after the
further suffering under Herbert Hoover in
1933. He was a wealthy man himself from an
aristocratic family but took it on as a
responsibility for the aristocracy to stem the
suffering of the masses. He instituted New
Deal government funded work programs and
social welfare that would help to stop the
immense suffering from the Great Depression.
These New Deal programs gave those with work
skills avenues to help contribute to society.
He also enacted regulatory commissions to
control big business and make sure the

aristocratic class was looking out for the interest of all and not just themselves. Many of these program's still exist today such as the Securities and Exchange Commission, Federal Deposit Insurance Program and Social Security enactment. Franklin Roosevelt was a hero to the common man worker but was hated by the aristocratic classes as they felt he was withdrawing their monopoly on money and power in the United States. He instituted inheritance taxes which helped break up the monopolies that wealthy families would keep on American industry and life. Further government revenue was also generated to help fund social programs and other government ventures. This attack on the aristocratic class actually forced the wealthy to look out for the common worker and create jobs and working conditions that would help the United States dig its way out of the Great Depression. The wealthy as a result of the policies of the president were forced to look to new ways of gaining profits and invested in new industries that employed millions of the unemployed.

Unfortunately Hitler's expansion in Europe coincided with this period of growth in America. Initially America took a neutral stance to the war in Europe as the country was already dealing with the suffering from a recent economic depression. The attack on Pearl Harbor and the declaration of war by Hitler on the United States drew the country into a two front war. Immediately companies and industries that were in the production of war materials and goods were either contracted or nationalized to support the war effort. The unemployment rate dropped to 2% with all of the extra work available to build up for the war. Millions of Americans were enlisted to the armed services branches for the war. The war completely brought the United States out of the depression but ended up as the most deadly conflict ever in human history. The sudden spike in demand for war products created millions of new jobs among the defense sector and spiked the stock of defense companies. During World War Two American corporations experienced record profits and the unemployment rate was as low as the United States had ever seen. One must ask themselves why this is so; why is it that under our current societal and economic structure all out war brings success to everyone not directly involved in the fighting. Around 400,000 Americans were killed during the conflict. This is three times the population of my entire home-cities population. The total deaths globally are some 25 million service men and around 40 million civilians.

The reasons for this mass conflict have been studied by historians for much the last 75 years. It was ultimately a story of retaliation from previous wars and imperialism. After World War One Germany was never actually completely defeated but was convinced into a peace accord with ramifications for following international agreements post war. Germany was forced to pay for much of the cost of the war monetarily and the Deutschemark instantly became more valuable for burning as fuel than useful as far as the international community was concerned. The unemployment rate reached heights of 60% as disease and suffering ran rapid after the first war. All of the blame was centered on Germany as agitation for World War One. In addition, Germany still had a Dolchstoßlegende, German term meaning a feeling of being stabbed in the back by the international community. The once powerful and nationalistic Germany was driven to poverty. This state of Germany allowed for popular voices of distain against the international community for causing such suffering. It was a ripe situation for a chancellor in Hitler to take control over Germany. When he set up mass work camps and a new commitment to industrialism he was able to win the trust of the German people. Ultimately Germany arose from the ashes of World War One and sought to take back the power the German empire once had. Throughout World War Two they would commit some of the most heinous war crimes ever in history as an effort to spread pure German nationalism. World War Two on this front arose out of economic devastation.

Japan was also a nation that displayed nationalistic behavior with strict military control and government of its people. Japan was a nation akin to Hollywood films on ninjas and Japanese culture. Industrialization did not yet hit Japan as they were able to run an efficient society off of classical culture. Shoguns, which were the head of the clan of warriors, retained political control over the region they saw over. The Emperor of Japan had final say over political matters. Japan was very isolationist and did not permit access to ports of Japan by sea except to very few traders including some Dutch and Chinese traders. The U.S navy sailed on Japan with steamboats mounted with hundreds of modern cannons and guns. They forced a meeting with the Emperor and opened up trade and dialogue starting in the late 1850s. From this time on Japan struggled with maintaining its' love for its' traditional culture and joining the ranks of industrialized nations. The feeling of being marginalized in world affairs has been said to contribute to Japan's aggression once industrial status was reached. The extreme nationalism and pride that Japan had for thousands of years was questioned when confronted with these new industrial nations that would seek to control and exploit a once great Japan. Japan developed a modern navy and army under the direction of other nations but turned against previous adversaries such as Russian, China and eventually the United States to establish a great and powerful Japan.

Not just the world wars but many conflicts in recent history have been a result of the imperialism of more developed nations and the retaliation of exploited people groups. This is another huge theme of the late 19th 20th century that is paramount to understanding embedded reasons for historical events and modern events. This imperialism displayed by many countries either caused the exploited countries to rise up in conflict or it even creates conflict among two competing countries who both seek to exploit a given region. This selfishness and disregard for nations and people groups that were less developed during the industrial spike in the world caused a lot of suffering.

This idea mixed with nationalism creates major problems with global relations. When everyone feels they are the best and everyone else is somehow less human, it can lead to mass unrest in the world along with the fact that they will seek out self interest at the expense of conflict. Another problem with foreign relations is the Anarchic international system which means that when any disagreements occur there are not too many organizations that can intermediate relations between two nations who both have self interest at stake. Once talks break down the next step is military action on part of both countries. As you can see, international conditions at some points are ripe for conflict especially when there is territory and resources that may be up for grabs around the world. The strong industrial nations fight over the resource rich more classical countries and from the perspective of the indigenous person there are multiple empires trying to exploit you. Many nations have turned entire populations into slave workers. The odes then lie on the selfishness displayed by humans who have attained privileged positions in the world. This helps explain historical events up to this time period. World War Two ended in catastrophic fashion as two nuclear bombs were dropped on Japan in Hiroshima and Nagasaki where hundreds of thousands of civilians were incinerated in seconds. Russia overwhelmed Germany from the East and the United States marched in from the West to take Germany and find Hitler who had poisoned him and his wife before the invasion. Germany was carved into two spheres of influence with Russia controlling East Germany and the United States and the West controlling West Germany.

This started the ideological cold war
between the west and eastern world. This clash
of ideals was among one of the most
fundamental ideal clashes that has permeated
this earth for most of history. Like I
explained, the clash between an aristocratic
privileged class and the masses has been a
forefront in human relations in many societies
for all of history. This clash took a complete
ideological form with the Eastern world taking
heed to Karl Marx's writing on equality and
the class of the masses taking economic power
as a democracy over the elite ruling class.
The west stuck to its philosophy of free
enterprise and individual entrepreneurial
rises to the aristocratic class. The west
would develop stories in Hollywood and in
print of individuals capitalizing on
opportunity and reaching wealth and
prosperity. The east saw this as a way of
conditioning the masses to except their
current state as a laborer in a mass society.
Feeding stories of meteoric rises of lower
class individuals would keep the lower classes
working hard and in constant pursuit of
reaching higher. While the lower classes did
that the bourgeoisie class would keep getting
wealthier and keep the same power structure
already in place. This led to a very hostile
view of the United States from the perspective
of the East. They felt the United States was
even bad for its own citizens therefore they
displayed aggressive foreign policy which
escalated the United States defense policy and
in turn resulted in the nuclear arms race. The
United States defense policy would be to
contain communism and not let it spread. Our
government and elite would frame the results
of communism as an attack on individual

freedom and liberty. Any military action taken by the United States to contain communism was framed as a campaign to defend freedom and liberty in the world. Ideological propaganda was produced explaining how under communism no individual can rise above the collective and that your freedoms will be limited by the state. The Eastern propaganda explained how you would be held down economically by the elite and ultimately lose your freedom to wage slavery in which you are owned by whatever elite class your business serves. War propaganda was a huge industry and fueled public support for military action in Korea to contain communism. At the same token the ideas of spreading Marxism fueled young men in Russia to go on campaigns to free exploited classes from various countries around the world.

The first major conflict resulted from the North Koreans invading South Korea with the support of communists in South Korea. The United States was granted control of South Korea south of the 39th parallel after World War Two. Korea actually had a movement of the people towards communism and then was funded by the U.S.S.R to help invade South Korea. The United States at an Elite level realized this was a major spread of the ideas of communism represented in a country uprising. They would not see this happen as the defense policy was to fight communism wherever it rises in the world. General Mac Arthur led an invasion force which initially drove the North Korean forces north but meanwhile China had attested to the action as a ploy of the United States to attempt to invade China. They ended up getting involved in the war and infiltrated

hundreds of thousands of forces pushing down
from China and drove back Mac Arthur back to
the initial borders drew up after world war
two. Hundreds of thousands were killed in this
conflict along with another couple hundred
thousand in Vietnam which looks remarkably
similar to the Korean War except we completely
pulled out of Vietnam at the end of the
conflict.

Vietnam was the first all out media war
where depictions of the warfare were readily
available by print or television. In
Universities and groups throughout the nation
protests against the war took place in
tremendous fashion. The 60's and 70's in
America resemble something like the
enlightenment period in Europe where normal
citizens consider the impact of the society
and rules of society that they live in. Many
new ideas arose out of this era. The
conditions of society were ripe for
contemplation of the current system and why
things happen as they do. The ideological
conflict between communism and capitalism
manifested itself into elite driven military
conflict. The sheer terror that was displayed
on the national media to American viewers
caused contemplation among the most hardened
citizens on whether this war was the right
thing to do. Photos were on display of mass
civilians slaughtered by modern war weapons.
Women and children were mowed down as a side
effect of two groups of men engaging in brutal
warfare. Like I said, this caused a
psychological impact on Americans that arose
real decent against the effort. Most
considered the fact that war could not be
tolerated in a modern world with such

technology but others sought deeper answers to questions as why are we in conflict with communism and why do the elite seem to have outright power to decide such huge decisions in world affairs. As I have tried to point out this is not just a modern conflict it is a very old conflict among societies internally that has played out in so many harsh fashions throughout global history. Countries in the world have limited jurisdiction and because of this some in the society may wish to expand and conquer to provide more territory and power for a society. Some in the society may be more apt to aggression as a form of obtaining power. You can see this even among young children in school. There are bullies who use force as a way of obtaining social dominance and power, others obtain power by social alliances and some simply play fair and take what life gives them. This same concept can be applied to countries which are simply organizations of people with the same temperaments as the people who reside in them. The only variable is that different political systems result in different people among society making influential decisions when matters of war, conflict and social justice. In a monarchy with a royal family, regardless of the sentiment among the public an action of war will be taken by the country.

V.

In a true Democracy the people of the country would make the final decision. In a Republic, the people elect officials to represent them and they then have the final decision in matters of war. The United States

is a Democratic Republic in terms of our
political system. This means that we elect
officials to represent us in government. This
is not a true democracy as there are many
other factors that affect the will of the
people transitioning onto government action.
Officials are elected into the House of
Representatives and Senate at local levels.
These elections are at not as high profile and
do not receive as much media attention. The
dates are not the same every year for one
thing and most of the time they are held on a
weekday where many Americans may have prior
obligations preventing them from voting. The
voting system caters to those who already are
in some sort of elevated position where they
easily can take time off or have even the
transportation to get to polling locations.
This is evidenced by the staggeringly low
turnout rates at gubernatorial elections. The
point to all of this is that in America it is
not the masses that make important decisions
such as invading Vietnam it is elected
officials who may have been elected by a slim
portion of elite. To declare war a 2/3rd
majority must be reached in the House and the
Senate. Once in office, House and Senate
members must raise donations for new terms
office. They might be beholden to people who
have elite status and money and might be
skewed to serve interests other than the
people. Therefore in some circumstances our
Democratic Republic system may lead to Elite
being in control of government. This was at
the front of the conflict among society in
Vietnam era America. Masses felt they were
being dragged into endless military conflict
and economic despair at the elite's whim. The
elite, Government and those who had a vested

interest in the war such as family who was serving saw these people as traitors who did not support the cause at hand. Again these elite versus the masses conflicts arise out of great societies. Many things can be explained by this concept. Families and organizations who get ahead economically institute policies and ways of organizing society so that they may maintain their superiority in economics. These very privileged people after years of success see an opportunity to widen their control on power and economics and use the masses to create armies to fight for their interests. Just as a child or a competitor may get too confident in their abilities, this happens on the societal level with elite who feel that can take more power and wealth then they are capable of.

When they overreach and cause military conflict millions can die or be affected. 99% of conflicts in history have resulted in both sides maintaining their current status or one massacring the other side but eventually down the road it comes back around and hits them back with a very blunt force. The downfall of many great societies including the likes of Rome, Athens, Sparta and many others can be explained by, first of all greed among the elite that leads to economic devastation, and also greed on the part of military action to take on more territory and power but being destroyed in the end by either death by force or disease. The sad part is that sometimes the elite can make it out of these disasters untouched but it is the masses who suffer endlessly from the whim of the elite who overreach their greed and desire for power. The common story of the end of a great civilization is the economic bankrupting and unemployment that is caused by the greed of the elite and then the dismantling of organizations because of the lack of money. This combined with over reach of war are recipes for collapse. War also helps bankrupt countries while the elite grab whatever wealth is left from the masses and this leads to complete collapse. As you can see the 60's and 70's were a time of the masses rising up against the elite and the elite trying to squash their movement. This exemplified some of the most unstable decades in American history. Voices of dissent in America maintained very, very strong opinions against the war. One American even copied the martyrdom displayed by a Monk in Vietnam who held a sacred position while burning alive in the town square. One man's quote from the Vietnam era exemplified the feeling of those against the war: Felix Greene

> *The mounting fury of the richest and most powerful country is today being directed against one of the smallest and poorest countries in the world. The average income of the people of Vietnam is about $50 a year - what the average American earns in a single week. The war today is costing the United States three million dollars an hour. What could not the Vietnamese do for their country with what we spend in one day fighting them! It is costing the United States $400,000 to kill one guerrilla - enough to pay the annual income of 8,000 Vietnamese. The United States can burn and devastate; it can annihilate the*

Vietnamese; but it cannot conquer them.

To dissenters it seems no matter what logic you use against the war the elite and government will explain that we must not let communism spread. Even with such atrocities during the war that many compared the napalming of Vietnamese by Americans on the same level as war crimes committed by Nazi Germany. This era was hugely defined by these questions. To give my overview of why the elite and government distained communism I simply have to point to the fact that under capitalism, elite and wealthy individuals are celebrated and their behavior is reinforced. Under communism equality of classes is paramount and elite and wealthy are seen as a poison in society that is keeping the society as a whole from progressing. The spread of the ideas of Marx would lead to the downfall of the elite and wealthy. Given the Elite and wealthy control power structures in a Democratic Republic they would have an extreme incentive to fight communism's spread. The masses might be indifferent but the wealthy see it as the single threat against their extremely privileged way of life. This is why such irrational behavior was displayed during cold war conflicts. The elite and government were scared that they would be sucked down to the life of a normal citizen. They would exploit and murder to keep communism from spreading. I am not saying communism would be a better system for the United States but that during the Cold War elite feared the spread of communism so much so

that they would violate international
treaties and murder on demand to fight it
off. On top of this they would chastise
anyone in our own country against the war
efforts. Many were imprisoned during this
time period and some were killed in cold
blood with the most famous occurrence
being the Kent State riots where
civilians were gunned down by the
National Guard during mass protests.

VI.

It is hard to understand the reasoning
behind actions during conflicts when
looking through a historical lens but
when you try to understand the emotions
and tensions of the time you can see how
the elite and wealthy would at all costs
protect their way of life and how the
masses would see such needless
devastation and murder as intolerable.
Others, among the elite and military
would become so hardened to the realities
of war that they would talk about war in
such a light that it seems like a game, a
game to be won. The harsh realities of
the war would be realized by most,
however, after the withdrawal from
Vietnam. The government officially
created a law that would cap the amount
of time our armed forces could be in a
conflict to 90 days before having to
reach a vote in the House and Senate.
This would make it very hard to carry on
self interested limited wars like Vietnam
without majority approval first. Common
language in legislation of war changed as
a result of the War. Use of the United
States military would never be used

unless it was in defense of a foreign attack and would not call it into action to alter foreign affairs. This resulted from the devastation that was seen during the war and the media and mass public outcry against it. The United States was actually internationally condemned for war crimes against humanity for the My Lai massacre which was the mutilation, rape and murder of up to 500 Vietnamese civilians including women and children. The use of chemical weapons such as Agent Orange also was in violation of the Hague Convention on international law.

Post Vietnam War America inspired many unique movements among people. Free love and civil rights along with more of appreciation of daily life arose out of this era. This so called Hippy era was a movement of peace and love among humans in America. Focus on the finer things in life rather than competition and materialism was important to this movement. After the devastation and senseless killing visible for anyone to see on nightly news people reached for a more meaningful life than what has been going on in the world. Drugs did get involved with this movement but did not define it. Post war economics signaled a move of many Americans from the collective lower class to a newly visible middle class. This brought many Americans out of the activism that was prominent after Vietnam. Towards the end of the 1970s and 80s middle class America was the new focal point. Many Vietnam era protestors and hippies settled down with families and moved to the suburbs. This

era on a macroeconomic scale signaled the
shift of economics from a Keynesian model
of capitalism, which has government
direction and funding direct market
economies, to a neo-liberal approach
which is simply a hand's off approach to
the market. This happened in many
industrialized economies as the middle
class developed they got in part what
previously was held for the elite. Their
jobs would pay a living wage in which
they could afford the American dream of a
home and a few cars and vacation time
without long working hours. Deregulation
of economies allowed capitalists to
engineer new ways of profiting off of
markets that may be questionable morally
but with no regulation is fair game.

When the elite and wealthy made money
the middle class grew. The middle class
became a voting base for politicians who
would keep power structures and economics
working for these classes. There still
was a significant majority of lower class
workers in America but there were enough
middle class families who would vote for
the policies that would keep them in the
middle class in order to continue these
trends. The middle class kept growing
throughout the 80s as free trade
agreements were reached among our
neighboring and foreign countries. Free
trade between these countries and ours
means that manufacturers can build their
products in these countries at much lower
labor costs while being able to sell them
at home without huge tariffs and fees.
This began the manufacturing flight to
other countries. This was a nightmare for

the unskilled worker in the United States but a godsend to those who were in management or ownership of any number of American companies. They could find endless cheap labor without dealing with Unions or government regulation. Their profit margins skyrocketed and created a spike in the aristocratic class in the 80s and early 90s. On the opposite side unskilled workers experience economic hardship and despair. With policies blatantly geared for the wealthy in government it seemed there was nowhere to turn for these people and organized crime and drugs proliferated to fill the void for these people. All of this bottlenecked into a major stock market recession by the end of the 1980s and early 90s until the technology boom occurred which created more jobs. Other things such as the OPEC embargos on oil contributed to downturns in the economy as gas prices skyrocketed. Under George Bush senior's leadership the countries focus turned again to foreign affairs after being isolationist from the lessons learned from Vietnam. At this time the sting of the reality of war has faded and America again began to exude confidence and nationalism. George Bush created a rally around the "flag trend" in America, which is just a term in political science that explains how leaders can inspire nationalism among countries by using the symbol of the flag and previous wars to instill patriotism. Many academics were hired by, for all intensive purposes war mongers, to explain how Vietnam was simply a loss because of the unpatriotic views of citizens at the time. They blamed it on the media showing the war on television which decreased support for the war.

George Bush inherited a very conservative and elite driven Congress and House which allowed him to pursue foreign policy initiatives that are in the United States' self interest. This all led to the step in of the United States in the Gulf war in which we pushed back the Iraq military from Kuwait. It was a victory for the United States but more so political scientists saw it as a simple retreat by Iraq and if a localized war broke out we could have experienced another Vietnam-like conflict, not to foreshadow to our current situation. In a famous quote by George Bush senior he voiced "We have finally kicked the Vietnam syndrome". This perceived victory and the collapse of the U.S.S.R, due to elite exploitation and economic depravity, heralded the U.S into a new era of extreme nationalism and pride. We proclaim that we are the best country in the world at many events including sporting events in which we were dominant such as the sport of basketball in international competition which leads to even more national pride. The early 90s were a time of prosperity for many as the middle class has expanded. The 90s saw economic growth because of the technology boom with computers, cell phones and all sorts of consumer electronics. This generation was defined by pop culture and icons. The middle class maintained and the lower classes continued to live in

poorer urban areas working very low
paying jobs supporting the upper classes.
There was a lot of stereotyping and
chastising of the poor as the idea of
pulling yourself out of poverty became
the norm. It is arguable whether a lower
class individual could really accomplish
this. The idea of equal opportunity was
really coined during this decade. Many
who did not rise up into the middle class
were blamed for their own laziness and
inability to work hard. Overall, however
the 90s brought one of the most
prosperous decades and was an example of
the best that our political and economic
system can offer in the world.

VII.

   A shift occurred at the end of the
decade that would start to bring down the
prosperous system that was somewhat in
place. The 80s started the transition to
globalization of business. General labor
jobs were outsourced to Mexico, Canada
and other Asian countries. To fill the
void of this many middle class positions
in companies were offered and actually
brought many from the lower class to the
Middle class. The shift that turned us
towards the economy we experience today
is that in the 90's companies began to
tighten their belts in search for more
profits. Middle class positions were
filtered out of companies and all that
would be left by our modern day is
management and ownership along with the
foreign labor. As all companies did this
they single handedly eliminated millions
of jobs from the economy. With the

dwindling of the middle class in a capitalist economy there became much less consumers who would purchase items from American corporations and the pyramid then began to fall in the economy. No money was circulating to corporations which led to even more layoffs and further retraction of the economy. Those with no money simply did not have the money to be consumers and those with money would save it as they feared for times ahead. In a capitalist economy the exchange of money around corporations and consumers is what keeps it alive. While all this was occurring one of the largest non-state attacks on the United States occurred on September 11th 2001, which shook the minds and confidence of many Americans. It had been so long since the United States has been up close with any war-like conflict. It was such a shock coming out of the prosperity of the 90's to see ourselves as unable to stop an attack on such a scale. It was almost a flashback to Vietnam era America as we all were glued to our television screens watching as people jumped to their deaths and the buildings fell on thousands of Americans. This attack seemed to strike fear into many Americans as nobody expected or could imagine such an occurrence on American soil.

The origins of the terrorist group headed by Osama Bin Laden cross into some very influential cold war occurrences. It started with the Soviet invasion of Afghanistan to help prop up the communist uprisings. In response to this, the defense policy of the United States to fight and contain communism enlisted that we fund the Mujahideen with weapons and cash to help fight the Soviets. Osama Bin Laden was part of a wealthy family that would allow him to be the funding for the uprising against the Soviets and communists. The Soviets' experience in Afghanistan actually looks remarkably similar to ours. They occupied Afghanistan for 10 years and experienced many casualties from disease and guerilla warfare against the Mujahideen. They attempted to prop up a puppet communist regime to maintain stability within Afghanistan but only ran into more problems as time went on. After the withdrawal of troops by the Soviets and the subsequent dismantling of the U.S.S.R the Mujahideen and the Afghan rebels experienced great pride and nationalism. They felt as though they had a hand in eradicating the Soviets and dismantling the ability for them to display imperialism while also forcing a form of Westernization onto Muslim territory. This new invigorated nationalistic Mujahideen would influence politics and society in Afghanistan and other Muslim countries around the Middle East. The Muslim religion took on a new pride attached to political relations as it was seen as the determining factor to pushing out the Soviets. Militant groups sprang up from around the Middle East as organizations whose purpose was to spread the fundamentals of the Muslim religion to the world much like the Soviets, attempted to spread Marxism. This stew of Muslim hard lined Soviet invasion era fighters that organized themselves into religious groups came to be known as the Taliban. Over the following decade they would be more and more isolated and stringent as many hard lined fundamentalist groups do. Eventually groups such as these lose focus on the outside world and seem to dehumanize those who do not belong to their world view. They began to target the western world as the number one problem to be solved. The idea would be to spread Muslim values globally. Using military force is not directly written in the Koran just as using force to spread Christianity is not directly written in the Bible. There are those however such as the Taliban that contort the writings of holy books to fit their ambitions. The Mujahideen, after the success of the military rebellion against the Soviets now intertwined force with their message of the Muslim religion. They organized violent acts around the Middle East especially focusing on the intersection of the western world with the Middle East in Israel. As these uprisings developed networks of people and resources developed and wealthy members of oil tycoons became the funders of these groups within the Middle East. Osama Bin Laden became one of the marquee funders and planners of the network of groups in the Middle East. A series of attacks on the western world were planned as an attempt to dismantle the United States just as they felt they had done to the U.S.S.R. As we all know they used passenger airliners to hit the United

States in strategic Mecca's such as the
International Trade towers and the
Pentagon. Just as they had felt the
prophet Mohammed willed the Afghan
rebellion to push out the Soviets the
Taliban felt at the direction of their
God they would topple the western power
structure in the world and bring about
Muslim values globally. This completely
clouded their moral conscience on the
values of individual human life as their
actions caused the deaths of thousands of
innocent Americans and heroes who
responded to save those in the twin
towers.

The George Bush administration elected
a plan that would seek a very hard lined
policy to root out terrorist cells and
any country that harbors terrorists. We
chose to attack countries on a political
level that harbored terrorists instead of
going after individual terrorists alone.
A rally round the flag mentality
signified post 9/11 where a new sense of
American pride but also vulnerability
resulted in thousands of men and women
enlisting to protect America and our way
of life. These men and women enlisted in
the idea that they could protect and
ensure our way of life. The intentions of
the service men and women were nothing
more than admirable it is just the
circumstances they are put in and the
direction provided by elite in government
that I will examine. The Taliban were
localized groups in Afghanistan and did
have some influence in government through
bribes and lobbying. They were not part
of the government. Their power rested in

the fact that they had secured weapons from the Soviet conflict that were funded by the United States. They maintained stock piles and held them at the headquarters of Taliban organizational compounds. The government of the United States had a few options of what to accomplish with military intervention. They could execute a small scale intervention in which small groups of military personnel could go after targeted leadership of the Taliban and capture them dead or alive to answer to their crimes or they would launch a wholesale invasion to Afghanistan and try to accomplish what the Soviets did by propping up a puppet government and try to instill western style government onto the Afghan people. The George Bush defense administration chose to attempt to defeat the Taliban and take over the government and put into place a western style Democratic Republic government. This meant large amounts of U.S forces and resources were required for a wholesale invasion plan. This whole plan ended up eerily similar to the Soviet occupation plan. When we occupied Afghanistan many in the country remember back to the perceived imperialism that the Soviets displayed and rallied support to try to throw out yet another western power. Needless to say this caused the endless uprisings and guerilla warfare that our troops experienced. It became a horrible conundrum of American soldiers set out to protect us being gunned down by the citizens they feel they are liberating.

The whole conflict became a brutal and emotional battle where it seemed like the entire Middle East was a plague. This war sentiment and zeal to conquer this area and implement our way of life spurred support for a second invasion in Iraq to topple Saddam Hussein who invaded Kuwait and started the first Gulf War. The combined effort in Afghanistan and Iraq is set as a plan to introduce western ideals into the Middle East and civilize one of the perceived danger pockets in the world. This set the objectives in the Middle East to be long term occupation and nation building to build a beacon of light in what we view as a dark world. Now, in 2011 we are still occupying both nations and we still experience uprisings from various groups among the two countries. The government officials we place in power become targets of the people and on many levels the structure of the newly formed government and military seems to dissolve just when stability seems possible. We have lost thousands of American soldiers in what seems to be a never ending struggle. The Afghans and Iraqis have lost thousands if not hundreds of thousands of fighters and civilians in the conflict. Again, I am not questioning the heroism of American soldiers but I do question decisions by the elite to enter into such a grandiose mission that has been tried and failed by many. The operation which is perceived to be imperialism by the citizens of Iraq and Afghanistan feel as though their culture and lifestyle is being stolen from them by the western world. At the same time the misunderstandings we experience with the Middle East only leads to a growth of hostility and hate among the people which can only lead to more suffering.

All the while in the first decade of the 21st century our domestic experience has tumbled into an economic recession in which by real accounts of unemployment and poverty have rivaled the first Great Depression. Trillions and trillions of dollars have been spent on our two front occupations and consumer confidence has completely declined as people begin to save and not spend leading to declines in corporate sales which then eliminates jobs. All the while, the banking system is collapsing under its own weight. The masses have experienced income reductions while corporate profits maintained and banks began to loan money to the masses at a rate similar to the Roaring Twenties before the Great Depression. Any profits that decreased because of consumers not spending were made up for by interest payments from the masses. However, when the masses began to experience unemployment and not just income reduction, mass amounts of people began to default on loans. Beginning with the housing mortgage industry, the banking system completely bankrupted itself and required the largest bailout from the United States government in history. We now have a president who sided with the masses for one of the first times in American history but also has a strong right wing movement of elite and wealthy who will at all costs protect their self

interest in America. A massive government
debt and unemployment number rivaling the
Great Depression coincide with efforts to
stimulate the economy by the government
through Keynesian economic spending and
also a Republican agenda which seeks to
eliminate social welfare for the masses
to save money and bring back an era of
Elite dominance in society. The issue of
the Elite exploiting the masses has been
brought up significantly in society. The
Elite and right wing politicians have
become desperate to turn the discourse
away from the struggling of the masses to
the collective power of the U.S to
continue to spread our way of life and
capitalistic industrialism to the rest of
the world. All the while many suffer as a
result of the crash of our economy and
many seek to exploit this climate to turn
more profits and build more power.
History and society do not happen by
accident; the rules, concepts and the
focus of power that originate in a
society cause outcomes and also influence
affairs inside a country. Many different
modes of society have been tried, tested
and philosophized in human history. As we
experience such hardship from our way of
life in the United States, people begin
to look to other modes of society and
economics that can help bring the United
States and the world out of its current
state.

The World in Our Hands

Adam M. Yeoman

The History and Categorization of Political and Economic Thought

*T*he spectrum of political and economic views in the history of our world is extremely broad. In today's age we attempt to classify political and economic views on an ideological spectrum line which constitutes the left and right in politics. The current political divide is then a result of one party's views moving further to the right and the other party moving to the left on the political spectrum. As the space increases in the divide it becomes harder and harder to cooperate. This ideological divide is what causes stark disagreements on political issues in government. Even issues that are seemingly non-important become a platform for intense arguing and idea debating. This ideological divide is the pinnacle of two dividing thought patterns in society for thousands of years. Our American political spectrum is more

limited than the spectrum of world history but
contains the Right in politics which the
Republicans value and the Left which the
Democrats adhere to. American politics can be
divided into views on social issues and
economic philosophy. The social view of the
Republican Right consists of Christian
fundamentalist views on morality. Family
values and Christian ethics make up the social
views of the right in America. The social
views of the Left in America consist of the
liberalism of lifestyles. Moral relativity and
acceptance of those different than you make up
a large portion of the social views of the
politics of the Left. The separation in views
on social issues does cause arguments ranging
from the issues of gay marriage, abortion,
drug policy and many others. The strictness of
the Republican policies has led our nation to
incarcerate more of our population for non-
violent crimes than any other nation in the
world or even in history. Some classic
policies of the Left include the passage of
gay marriage rights in certain states and the
right for a woman to choose on matters of
birth control.

Economic policies are what are at stake in
the national debate. The divide in economic
policies is huge and almost reconcilable given
the types of differences in philosophies and
the agendas of both parties. The economic
policies of the Right take heed from past
political philosophers from Europe. Thomas
Hobbes, Nicholas Machiavelli, Adam Smith and
John Locke make up most of the prominent
thinkers who influenced the ideology and
policies of the Republican Right. The ideology
of the Left in America is actually very

conservative relative to the views in history and globally that are inspired from the writers who have influenced economic and political policies. Major influences include Plato, Jean Jacque Rousseau, Karl Marx, John Maynard Keyes and many others. The economic ideology and politics in the United States is actually very moderate when compared to the range of possible economic and political organizations that have been tried by humans. The extent that we drift to the Right in politics and economics is the lobbying of religious groups who create laws and statutes that reflect Christian ideals. Economics becomes limited by the ideals of Christianity by stifling scientific discoveries such as stem-cell research and other genetic manipulations. A strong military is advocated to help protect a home for Christianity and sometimes use force to liberate other areas that we feel may be oppressed by another way of culture. An example of a far Right society is the Middle-Ages in Europe where effective secular government was pretty much eliminated in favor of a Church aristocracy that ruled on the laws provided by the Church and the Bible. The economics in the United States on the Right keep power in the hands of the business owners and managers who are predominantly white Christians who have held on to industry since the early founding of the United States. The free market then decides the wages paid to laborers. The '9 to 5' work week and Church on Sundays along with strict marriage keeps people in line with the Christian views of the world. The Left side of the political spectrum is also relatively moderate compared to what exists and has existed in the rest of the world economically and politically. Our debate in America for economics and politics is an argument between Keynesian economics to help keep the market working for the people as a whole and not just the wealthy. This is done by using the government's power and resources to regulate industry and stimulate job growth by inserting money into the market where needed. A good metaphor is that the government simply makes a few modifications and repairs to a train and then puts it back on the tracks. The argument of the Left does not take away the free market and the laissez-faire approach; it simply adjusts it to make sure it is running properly for everyone and not just the few. Again, this is actually very moderate thinking relative to other economic theories that have been thought of and tried. Most of Europe runs on the philosophy which is what the Democrats are pushing, a social market economy. It is a market economy that works for the betterment of all people in the society. If you go even further to the Left in history such as with the U.S.S.R there was the complete elimination of the market and money. It was socialism on a national level with no organized religion and everyone cooperating for the betterment of all.

II.

This was a very broad overview of some of the different modes of economic and political theory but the fact is that each of these theories and way of life have permeated in society somewhere and history along with great minds have philosophized on the merits. To look at each of these individually in their context will help to understand how each raises outcomes in society that are purposefully put there or happen as a side effect of the societal theory. Some of these philosophers have been implemented into real societies and others are simply influences on societal organization. The early philosophers on society and human interactions include Plato, Socrates and Aristotle. Plato's views were very broad and in a way set up the discussion by humans about concepts such as the nature of Justice and man's relation to the world. He inspired major concepts that are still in action today. Even the concept of philosophy was in some way coined by him. He philosophized on mans relation with himself and his relation to others in society. Plato also originated ideas of mans relation to the divine. His major premise split mans soul into different parts and stages of development. Some men want a simple and honorable life and fit into a category of a stable soul. Others have the soul of a fighter or warrior who has harnessed the power of the soul as relation to the forms but has not taken up the understanding that comes with it. The philosopher is then one of which takes power from the forms and uses it to understand justice on every level including within them. This is the state in which a man has conquered the idea of 'self' and thinks of the justice that pertains to all people instead of self interest.

Plato's theory of the forms has to do with man's ability to shape reality. Technology and production have created objects and things that are not of nature. He believes a state of everything humans can do and achieve, exists in our pre and after life. During life the closer we get to the forms or surpass our human form where our soul can see past our physical lives. In this state things can be accessed from the forms and this is how humans are able to shape nature into things we use such as chairs, houses and technology such as computers and televisions. Plato's belief is that soul is from the divine and that the body has material attachments that influence the soul's behavior. The closer you are to accessing your true soul, the closer you are to discovering things that existed in your pre life. To Plato this would explain sudden technological advances. People who are closer to the forms are able to come up with discoveries that catapult human advances in science and technology. The forms are then an alternate reality where everything possible on earth is already done and human souls exist in the purest state. In some way just having this theory created the foundation for the Industrial Revolution that would follow much later. It also made the dualist idea of the soul and body popular.

The main premise by Plato is that Justice is what defines the happy life. Leaders must look out for the justice of all people and have a certain type of soul where they can see past their own personal self interest and see the common good of all people. Aristotle also influenced many modern ideas such as appealing to reason as a primary way of solving problems. The Scientific Revolution was attributed to the thought patterns created by Aristotle. Secularism and using scientific reasoning to solve problems was a superior way of solving world problems then by faith which was previously the norm. Many advances in society occurred after the switch from faith based reasoning to secular reasoning.

The irony of what actually occurred after
the implementation of the ideals of Plato and
Aristotle is that the secular reasoning of
Aristotle led to the way that industry is
organized in a very non-humanistic manner.
The ideas of Plato and justice were somewhat
abandoned for the new version of secular
materialism that became popular. This secular
humanism shifted man's thought that evil in
man comes from the devil to the fact that
humans just have evil in our nature and are
naturally self interested. This spawned
thinkers such as Thomas Hobbes and Nicholas
Machiavelli. Others answered back that with
secularism it is not humans that have evil in
their nature but it is simply a reaction to
imbalances in justice as described by Plato.
These injustices force men to do evil things
but are not inherently evil. Jean Jacque
Rousseau and others such as Karl Marx take
these views on the world.

III.

Thomas Hobbes believes that in the state of
nature without any political control man's
life would be, quote, "Nasty, brutish and
short". He believes strict political control
and rules are the only way to stave off mans
brutish nature. A leviathan that instills fear
and power must be present to keep humans
inline. He originated this realist view of
international relations where self- interest
and power are all that drive man's decisions.
He influenced Machiavelli who wrote strictly
on foreign relations of states. The idea that
self interest is moral even when it means
conquering another state was popular to him.
He believes if the other state is able to be

conquered they do not deserve to have control over their state, as they were too weak in the first place to be governing under the principles of Hobbes where strong leadership is the only thing keeping humans from being evil. As Thomas Hobbes and Machiavelli laid the ground work for an era of strong nationalism and military expansion Adam Smith wrote using these same theories about economics. He used these same principles of evil in human nature and the perceived psychology of man to come up with a theory of modern industrial economics. Adam Smith argued for the independence of national economies from government control. He wanted to take Europe out of Feudalism with royal control over economies to a variety of wealthy industry leaders taking power over their industry. It was a manifesto that actually attempts to give a moral ground for wealthy elite to seize power over the masses. The selfishness of the elite and men who control economies actually leads to economic growth for the masses. This is the famous reference to the trickle-down effect in economies that many Republican candidates go to. The argument in Adam Smith's manifesto is that man is naturally selfish and self interested. Therefore to cater to this state the economic system of man must benefit from man's selfishness. The origins of modern capitalism were invented from this philosophy. It became a manifesto to wealthy men who would dominate industry in the 18 and 19th centuries. They attributed what they did as an owner or manager to the fact that they are creating economic growth. Selfishness they displayed such as not paying employees a fair wage and making them work strenuous hours was chalked up to the fact that in the end there was economic growth. They justified selfishness and maltreatment with the philosophies of Adam Smith. As you can see, the Industrial Revolution was an effort by the elite to organize labor and use top-down power structures to organize mass factory and industrial labor in order to bring about a Revolution of world economics and technology.

In addition, economic and political theory can translate to common ways of doing things and result in effects on society. Adam Smith's manifesto resulted in modern capitalism as well as individuals making industrial advances while driving mass laborers to complete the work. Adam Smith was jealous of the power that was given to Royals and their appointed staff. He argued that if that kind of power could be in place in industrial sectors such as the farms and mills that this type of control would create more growth than simply a distant King or Queen mandating things from their thrown. This then over time shifted power structures of Royalty making decrees on economic productivity to various industrial wealthy leaders gaining control of the labor. This advent did create economic industrial booms of various new products and services in the world while at the same time it also wrecked havoc on workers' rights, wages and working conditions. The selfishness displayed by the owners and managers of labors was justified by Adam Smith's manifesto the Wealth of Nations. Any argument by the workers on their mistreatment resulted in them being labeled as lazy and impeding world economic progress. Some workers labored for 24 hours straight with little or no rest and very meager incentive. The Industrial Revolution as a whole can be surmised by looking to the theory of Adam Smith. He does bring up good ideas on how the division and specialty of labor can bring about the most efficient economic growth. Using automated machinery and labor tools became popular as an effect of Adam Smith's writing. To imagine a world without the efficient way of producing manufactured goods would be difficult. His ideas of selfishness also led to economic exploration.

Initially, taking advantage of local resources and labor was the limit to industrialism. After the ideas of selfishness and modern capitalism occurred many nations began to explore in hopes to find foreign resources and cheap or free labor to help advance industrialism and economics. The combination of Nicholas Machiavelli's theories on state interactions and Adam Smith's theory of economics led to the era you see in history where countries invade and colonize foreign countries for their resources and somewhat enslave the population to complete the manual labor it takes to harvest them. This is of course done with the use of force as prescribed by Machiavelli. This is the story of the advent of the Industrial Revolution until now. Countries with self interest and nationalism are out to expand territorially and economically. This created many inter-country wars and conflicts over third world territory with natural resources. This was done at the expense of the indigenous people of whom many were massacred or sold into slave labor. All of the suffering and slave labor around the world led to the wealthy nations experiencing record economic growth and prosperity while many poorer nations suffered at the whim of the wealthy, elite countries. If this sounds familiar it is; the struggle between the elite and the masses between people of one country is the same explaining factor for international relations among wealthy elite nations and the poorer exploited counterparts.

IV.

On the other side of the political argument was a series of writers who wrote a critical analysis and competing theory on economics and politics. These theorists were put into action in other non-western countries such as China, Russia and many others. In many modern European countries these ideals have also been implemented. Plato was one of the first philosophers and more importantly the first philosopher to come up with ideas of what the perfect society would be. His analysis on justice is still relevant even today. Like I mentioned earlier, Plato originated the concept of the Soul and different levels of understanding. His critique on society was somewhat relevant to both the founding of the initial ideas of capitalism and that of a more communal idea of society such as Communism or Socialism. In some ways both Capitalism and Communism originated from the same idea. Plato's ideas on the perfect society had two facets. His ideas on justice in the interactions of men in society meant that those who hold power must pertain to the type of soul that allows them to see the good of all and not the self interest of himself or his friends. The society then is in the constant pursuit of achieving justice as a whole for each individual. This was the origination of the idea of perfection in society and achieving social justice. He influenced many ideas of the Renaissance and later ideas coming out of the Dark Ages with writers such as Jean Jacque Rousseau and later Karl Marx. The other side of Plato's theory on society was an economic component that was a very modern idea. He believed that transitioning out of classical society in which everyone had to deal with every component of labor involved with surviving could be corrected. In a classical society each man was responsible for providing food, shelter, clothing and water for his family. The idea that Plato coined, which is completely relevant to the advent of modern society, is that each man or woman could specialize in their own trade of labor and also that sharing among people would lead to humans being freed from the limitations and labor that comes with providing everything for ones' family. This is completely relevant to modern Capitalism and Industrialism. When each human or organization of humans specializes in producing their own product and trade with others who do the same we can catapult economic growth and bring humans out of the age of extensive labor that was involved in classical society and life.

In this way Plato planted ideas of the modern capitalist world of corporations and world trade. On the other end of his theory he originated ideas that would lead to a search for justice on a societal level. Plato's ideas influenced later philosophers and were the inspiration for writings on the Industrial Revolution and that of a social revolution.

Those inspired by the social aspect of Plato's writings include the writers I mentioned Jean Jacque Rousseau, Karl Marx as well as many others.

In search for better ways of achieving justice and harmony on a societal level Jean Jacque Rousseau wrote a manifesto concerning the social aspects of humans and how they can fit into an organized society. In Rousseau's manifesto, the discourse On the Social Contract, he gives an answer back to other writers at the time who took a view of human nature as inherently selfish and that through force and control men can be forced to behave. He compares this state of society as an ode to slavery. If a man undergoes a personal realization to behave a certain way he will behave this way consistently without coercion and also without force being present. The change of behavior under coercion with man is only an ode to necessity and not out of free will. Rousseau appeals to the fact that one of God's laws is that of free will and not slavery. In mans natural state he will never operate as designed under the pretense of slavery. The theories that originated from the secularism of Aristotle and later by both Machiavelli and Hobbes violate one of man's natural rights. The term slavery can then be extended to incidences other than simply forced free labor. Coercion and force was once used to make men or women do something of necessity which is a violation of natural rights given to man under whatever sort of deity that was thought to create man. His objection to the societal theory of Machiavelli and Hobbes lends him to describe a theory of society based on the social aspect of humans and the ability to cooperate for the greater good.

Rousseau's replacement for the control that is instituted by a leviathan, using force and coercion to control and shape humans, is that of a social contract among humans. The idea Rousseau coined is that under a state of complete independence from other humans, man has to provide every means of survival for himself and this can be very strenuous. The idea is that instead of force and coercion to get humans to cooperate they will do this simply on their own free will when they realize the exponential benefit of living under a social contract and society. As Plato mentioned under the ideas of a perfect society, humans can be freed from providing everything for themselves and then focus on one thing that they do well and trade with others who do the same. The benefits of the Social Contract and the entrance into society from a state of nature make humans comply at their own free will. This to Rousseau is a much more longstanding commitment that will produce much greater results among a society.

The implications of this argument reach beyond a simple philosophical argument and extend into other areas. The clash of ideas between those who believe man should be controlled through force and coercion, and those who believe man should have the free will to determine whether they should contribute in a society, have arose in many areas such as the functions of government and the economic organization of countries. If you were to adhere to the idea that humans were naturally selfish and somewhat evil the correct form of government would be a stern bureaucracy with a strict legal code that instills fear in its citizens as a way of keeping them functioning in society. This strong handedness would extend down each level of government all the way down to the local court system and police. Economically you would use coercion and force to get people to labor in mass industrial complexes in order to better society as a whole. As you can see, the general idea of social institutions that regulate behavior among the country is that they would use strong handed techniques to control humans and keep them acting in a manner that is conducive to advancing as a society and a country. On the other end of the spectrum if you were to use Rousseau's theory he would believe that using force and coercion to get humans to act in line is a violation of their natural rights given to them by their creator. In some ways this is the beginning of the split between the Right and Left in politics. The Right in the United States uses tactics such as taking away social welfare so people are scared into working for them. They also institute very strict laws on public behavior and in some ways use a version of Christianity which instills fear of 'hell' as a way of controlling men. This same attitude is directed toward public policy and the workplace. I am not criticizing Christianity; I am simply attempting to show how theories such as that of Thomas Hobbes are put into practice. Again, Rousseau a religious man takes the view that coercion and force to control men is slavery and it is not how his 'God' uses his power.

V.

The way that 'God' uses his power and how men should organize society is convincing man to behave a certain way under his own free-will. Man will organize themselves into a civil society. The reason they would do this is because the benefits of being a member of the society far out-weighs that of being an individual with no help from anyone else but yourself. Therefore man does not have to be controlled; he simply has to be in a cooperative healthy society that he benefits from. There is no need to force masses to comply as they would do it on their own free-will for the benefit that they get from entering a Social Contract. In a system which Rousseau recommends there is no need for strict government and there is also no need for corporate elite who drive industry by the fear of being fired getting instilled in workers. Citizens would cooperate in a Democracy and pay taxes for the benefit that it brings and they would go to work for the benefit they receive also. They would not need to be coerced or forced to pay taxes and go to work. They would do it because without government they have no one to keep up public projects like roads and parks and they would go to work in a cooperative corporation to gain the benefit of industrialism. Like Plato mentioned, the cooperative work and trade can help create a perfect society. This will motivate citizens to cooperate and work on their own accord because as society progresses they themselves also progress.

This debate more so defines the modern American ideological debate than that of a fight between capitalism and communism. The idea that the Right in American politics has is that people must be coerced into working and contributing to society. They cling to this idea even when the facts of unemployment are pretty written in stone. In many areas of the country there are three or more people looking for a job per jobs actually available, meaning two or more people per job available will not find a job no matter how motivated they are. The idea among people who already own and manage businesses is that of the theory of Thomas Hobbes that these unemployed people must be coerced and forced back to work. Like I previously stated, these people also do not understand that no matter how much some of these people try they will not find employment when there are not enough jobs available for those looking. Combined with the fact that we have a national debt, the Right in politics seeks to use a solution prescribed by thinkers such as Hobbes. They need to cut government spending and will do this by attempting to cut social programs which help the unemployed and poor. They believe this is a reasonable thing to do as it will obviously make it extremely unbearable to stay unemployed. The fact though is that the number of jobs available is not enough to supply a job to everyone that is looking for employment as the numbers do not meet up. It would motivate some with coercion to find a job but others will not see such luck.

Putting Rousseau's argument into a modern conflict you can see how he would say these people want to contribute to society because of the benefit. The rest of society should be motivated to get these people back to work as it will contribute more goods and services to

all. It obviously benefits the person
receiving employment as they can then provide
for themselves and their family. The fight
then is between those who feel humans cannot
be trusted to behave and contribute without
coercion and those who believe these people
are simply on the losing end of a system that
will not let them succeed. You see this
ideological debate play out in modern politics
around the around and especially in the United
States. Any time someone from the thought camp
of Rousseau mentions anything about helping
the unemployed and underemployed the other
side accuses them of trying to institute
socialism which seems to be the worst thing
that could ever happen to them. To look closer
at what socialism actually is and what it
means will help explain the modern American
political climate. Many times in America
socialism is used as the same term as
communism.

These two concepts come from two different
philosophers and are in many ways completely
different. Jean Jacque Rousseau was the person
who came up with the main ideas of socialism
and other modern psychologists followed up on
his theory of society. Using psychology the
term socialism is described somewhat in terms
of what Rousseau did. There is an innate
psychological desire to cooperate in a society
to gain the outcomes you receive. Just as
Rousseau stated, people enter a social
contract to get out of the grueling life that
is an individual trying to make it on his own.
Most in America immediately correlate
socialism to a dictator controlling every
facet of your life. In many ways socialism is
the complete opposite, Thomas Hobbes who

believes humans need to be controlled believes in a dictator and him along with Adam Smith were the founders of the theory of economics we live under today. The confusion that Americans display has to do with the propaganda war that occurred during the cold war.

Communism as displayed in the former U.S.S.R was so demonized and hated in the American public media that just the sound of the word brings flashbacks to a time where drills took place in fears of a nuclear attack. Americans were instilled with immense fear by the propaganda machine in the United States. This explains a lot of the seemingly illogical proxy wars that were undertaken during the time period which saw an immense loss of American and foreign civilian life. The first thing to note about the U.S.S.R is communism arose out of a deadly civil war which across its' territory lost millions and millions of citizens to the violence. When Vladimir Lenin died, Joseph Stalin took his place and ruled with a stronger demeanor much like someone would if they adhered to the concept that man needed to be controlled for his own good; much like Thomas Hobbes mentioned. Many people believe the U.S.S.R was directly modeled after Karl Marx's theory of society and economics. In fact in the writings of Karl Marx the movement to obtain Communism is 'an effort to stomp out the bourgeoisie class and attain equal footing in society.' What happened in the U.S.S.R was a movement by the elite which is contrary to Marx's theory to force communism on peasants in Russia's territory and beyond.

The strong handedness displayed by the United Soviet Socialist Republic early on in its' history was not Communism but rather a military dictatorship attempting to force the ideas of Communism on a non-developed region of the world. As time went on and the region industrialized in some ways the U.S.S.R then did display the ideas of Marx in action and did see some prosperity. Again, the thing that bankrupted the U.S.S.R was the greed of the elite and the quest to spread Communism through military action.

As you can see these societal concepts can rear their influence in many different ways. It is then more understandable why the lines of these theories can be confused and take on much more meaning than the initial philosophy that originated the concept. Rousseau's theory can best be defined as Socialism and Marx's theory can be best described as masses rising up against elite who have monopolized the economic factors of production and use it as a way to control the masses. Communism is actually just an extrapolation of Marx's theory where after the masses take back control they attempt to keep everyone equal in social status. The many ideas thrown out to the American public about communism during propaganda wars with the U.S.S.R were ideas invented about communism. The clash between Capitalism and Marxism is then a whole new framework of ideology. The propaganda that was fed to the United States citizens has to do with the perceived idea of communism. The biggest arguments against communism were that an elite government would control everything you do and you would lose your free will and freedom in general. This does not sound

anything like Marx's theory but more so of
Thomas Hobbes' theory. It is completely
founded that people would not want this state
of economics and government. This is what the
early U.S.S.R displayed and it was treacherous
to the people of the region. This is not what
the Russian people strived for later on in
their society. They strived for equality and a
common goal of making the greatest union they
could to provide for all people under their
empire. They did not want a class structure in
their society with elite wealthy people who
use fear and their resources to control the
rest of the population. This was the idea of
Marx. The people of the U.S.S.R did not want
everyone to be exactly the same and display no
individualism and they also held to an
ideology that would eliminate the power
structures of fear and economic coercion that
the bourgeoisie could use with their
privileged position in society. The U.S.S.R
wanted to prove that their system was better
in such a way that the elite and selfish
people in government would bankrupt the
country at the expense of all the citizens of
the region. Again, Communism is the created
view of Marx's theory that Americans have of
the society displayed by the U.S.S.R.
Socialism is the idea displayed by Rousseau
which basically is the benefit that humans can
obtain by cooperating in society.

VI.

    In a social society there are different
ways you could solve problems such as
relieving unemployment. One solution could be
the commitment to private charity and simply

helping out the disadvantaged that you come in contact with. Another problem that happens to be going on right now in the United States is that some in our country confuse government spending to alleviate suffering with a dictatorial government as prescribed by Hobbes. In reality we are using the government as a tool of the public to help relieve the ills of society. Government is supposed to be a representation of the people manifested into an organization. What we are doing in the United States is using the combined power of our tax money to use it as a means to fund ways of relieving the suffering. Those who experience unemployment suffer as there are not enough jobs available for everyone in our society. This is what the definition of socialism in practice is; using the cooperative power of society we can either achieve great heights or help stop the suffering of the disadvantaged. It has nothing to do with the theory of Thomas Hobbes where elite are needed to control the masses and keep humans in line. At the end of the day if you believe that all humans are evil and could never cooperate on their own accord you would actually want strict control over society to keep good outcomes in the world. If you have faith in humanity to cooperate for the betterment of all you may see socialism as a way of achieving great things here on earth.

If you happen to be in a privileged status in the world you may experience extreme prosperity. The view from this position may be that those who are less fortunate may not have worked as hard or as intelligently as you may think you have in order to of gotten to where you are in the world. From the position of the person who is in a disadvantaged situation it may seem as it is impossible to rise above your current situation. Now there is an obvious disagreement where some believe that disadvantaged people are disadvantaged at their own fault and then you have the disadvantaged who feel it is the fault of the advantaged that they are in their current position. Many current economic and political arguments and discussions fall into this category. The ability to understand the direct causes of inequality and suffering would help in determining the proper actions to be taken by governments and relief organizations to help solve these problems. Understanding the reasons and beginnings of inequality in society is paramount in discerning what actions to take in order to solve the issues at hand. There are many philosophers who write on inequality and injustice in society. Jean Jacque Rousseau wrote a document philosophizing on the origins of inequality in human society. He separated the types of inequalities into physical differences which are present from natural evolution of species and that of which originates as a result of the organization of society. The differences between sects of humans' results in natural inequality which makes some men or women predisposed to succeed in certain areas. The physical ability and creativity of the mind are the most looked at natural differences among humans. Certain activities can highlight these natural inequalities. Physical activities such as sports rely on natural ability to determine the best athletes. Other activities such as art and certain fields such as engineering find the most creative minds which separate humans by natural ability.

Humans with very sharp minds and good memory would be predisposed to enter fields such as math and science. These are all natural inequalities which have everything to do with natural selections and genetics rather than the way humans organize themselves. These natural inequalities are also not completely set in stone as work and training can close the gap of inequality. The next form of inequality is what is of concern to philosophers and those who lead and organize society. The origin of inequality among man in his social status relative to other humans and his share of material goods is a more subjective question. Understanding human nature and how human's behaving absent of any society and control is important to understanding why inequality persists. Rousseau then examines the previous theories of the state of nature. The state of nature is how humans would behave before any society and technology. The reason for examining the state of nature is to find out about human nature so we can best organize society around this inherent nature of humans.

The general disagreement that Rousseau examines is that of the theory of Thomas Hobbes in which man is completely selfish and somewhat evil in absence of political control and that of other philosophers who think humans without political control may actually behave in such a fair fashion that it would resemble a utopia. The stance of Rousseau is somewhere in between these two ideas, he believes that man in a state of nature is out to fulfill self-preservation. Humans are not evil but they are concerned with their overall well being and because of this sometimes we

are forced to make choices that may hurt
someone else but maintain our way of life.
This idea of self preservation means that
humans are peaceful and naturally good when we
are not under the stress of losing out on
something in life. The evil in humans is then
the result of a conflict of interest when it
comes to something important that affects both
people's lives. The evil among humans is
enhanced when there is a conflict of interest
or a limited amount of a certain resource that
many people want or need. Life in the state of
nature can best be described as peaceful and
cooperative when resources are met but when
there is competition for resources or mates
then there are inherent stresses involved that
can make humans do irrational things such as
wage war. The general consensus is however, to
achieve a state of self-preservation for
yourself and elevate those around you to this
status to maintain stability in your life
among those you come in contact with. I tend
to believe this theory on human nature to be
the most accurate when looking at modern
hunter-gatherer groups living in remote
regions and also modern human behavior as
studied by psychology. This theory would make
it seem as though there would not be too much
inequality outside of natural inequalities
that are present from genetics.

VII.
    The question is why is there so much
economic inequality and social status
inequality in the world? If humans are out to
fulfill their own self-preservation and then
elevate others then why are there complete
social class divisions which separate
extremely wealthy individuals from the rest of

the world? This is probably one of the most complicated questions in human history. My theory on inequality has to do with the idea that the mental concept of self-preservation can change from person to person based on experiences and the information they have been drilled with from family and society. If someone's concept of what is a stable life to them is skewed by information that they receive then their idea of self-preservation may not be just having what you need but to be as extravagantly wealthy as possible. To illustrate this I will give an example of two peoples lives and how their ideas of what successful is and also self-preserving changes based on their surroundings.

Take a boy who grows up in a lower middle class neighborhood; his life and experiences consist of family life in which his father has a steady job that pays the bills and provides things that they need while also leaving some money left over for entertainment. This boy's idea of success from this point of view is growing up and starting a family while working at an honest job. He may have dreams of being a professional athlete or musician but realistically he strives for the life his parents had. This boy when he grows up would hope his friends can live the same life he does. He will seek his self-preservation which is attaining this life and once he does he would even commit time and money to help others reach this life if he could. This would tend to agree with Rousseau's theory of society and human nature. The next child grows up in a wealthy circle of friends and family. The father is a fortune 500 business owner and the wife is a socialite among the area. The child is raised to display the etiquette of that social group and be a perfectionist and leader at everything she does. She is expected to perform at the very top of her class in high school and get into the top university in the nation. She is then expected to obtain a leading role in a very important multi-national corporation out of college. Her idea of self-preservation is drastically different from the other child. The social pressure for her to succeed gives her completely different motives and aspirations than the child from the lower middle class family. Her idea of self-preservation is drastically different than the other child and it will make her attempt to achieve this ideal even if it might lead her to step on other people. Her idea of self-preservation is what is most important in her life as it is the foundation in which her life rests on. When she steps on people and turns her back on close friends to achieve her goals this does not make her an evil person; it makes her a person who does bad things with the intentions of living up to the standards she set for herself. She may attain a leading role for a world leading corporation and be faced with a choice of getting fired or demoted or laying off needlessly thousands of workers for the profit of the ownership group. She makes a choice to maintain her life the way it is which in turn causes others to suffer. As you can see sometimes difficult choices by people in power can carry much weight in what happens to others. In some circumstances people's ideas of self-preservation can be skewed and I feel this is a major contributor to the inequality among humans.

The issue of inequality and the ideas of how to stop inequality became so important that in the last century two world superpowers were almost brought to total war in disagreement of two sides of the argument on inequality and society. The United States stuck to the philosophy and practice of Adam Smith while the U.S.S.R maintained its views of Karl Marx. I have mentioned much on the views of Adam Smith but I will elaborate on the main ideas that the United States used as propaganda for the ideas of economic theory that the U.S elite maintain. The United States advocated in public discourse that the inequality in the United States is healthy and that those who have attained wealth have done it through hard work. It was also believed to be a model for the masses to work hard and maybe they will achieve that wealthy status in the future. The proliferation of the wealthy in the United States is also thought to have a trickle-down effect onto the rest of society where the wealth gained by the rich will trickle down to the masses. The selfishness displayed by the elite and wealthy is the main engine for economic growth. The class system in the United States is a way of instituting control over the masses and making them work hard for hopes of being wealthy in the future. In some sense this is a system that is taking advantage of the theory that humans need to be forced and coerced to contribute to society. These problems are a necessary effect of the system to those who preached on behalf of the American economic way. They showed the variety of different companies and consumer goods that the United States has a show of strength in this system. In America, inequality among humans has not been looked at to a very high degree. This is because our philosophy on economics believes that inequality is a way of fueling economic growth.

VIII.

On the other end of this argument you have the U.S.S.R whose entire economic and political system is based on the idea of stopping inequality. The ideas of Karl Marx spawned out of the maltreatment of the early Industrial Revolution in Europe and America. Karl Marx saw some of the worst human abuses in history being done in the light of day in various factories. Laborers were forced to work in some cases 24 hours a day to produce various products at the whim of management who profited immensely. Many people were killed on the job and others caught debilitating illnesses from the hazardous working environments. Children, women and others who were easily coerced were forced into even worse situations in factories as they would not stand up for themselves.

There was a strict division between ownership, management and the laborers. Laborers were paid pennies on the dollar that were earned by the company while ownership and management became wealthier than you could imagine. Once they became wealthy they attempted to join the aristocratic classes of Europe. Once in the aristocratic classes they were further separated from the struggle of those in the mass classes. They developed an attitude if they were responsible for the livelihood of their employees as if they were a ruler such as a king or queen. The ability to keep their employees working efficiently and hard only contributed to the monopoly of wealth and power that they have. All of these trends contributed to the division between the bourgeoisie and the working class that Karl Marx described in his manifesto. The bourgeoisie became a hereditary class of individuals who led privileged lives on the backs of average workers.

As time went on the distance between the two groups the Bourgeoisie and the working class became greater and a complete separation of values and ideals occurred. Those who were born into a family of the bourgeoisie would be groomed and educated to carry on the lives their parents had led. This in many ways was the origin of the modern university. Wealthy children would be put into elite universities and schools that would mark them as a business leader in the next generation. The ability to access this elite group by a working class individual became much harder as the monopolies on businesses and higher education were tightened. This is the why Karl Marx wrote on his philosophy, he grew up and experienced the blatant discrimination of the working class and the blatant elevation of privileged classes who had everything provided for them. The life of a working class individual seemed to be filled with countless hours of labor and the suffocation of hope. The wages workers were paid supplied them with the bare minimum housing available and enough food to survive. The prospect of vacationing or doing something for entertainment was almost impossible. The only entertainment available would be the company of family and friends. Work days were filled with tedious factory labor and a constant barrage from management appealing for faster and more efficient work. On the other side of things the management and ownership of these companies' days are filled with little or no actual labor but strategizing on ways of making the company and its laborers more efficient with the incentive that they will experience more and more profits. After "work" these people would dine in extravagance while planning their next vacation to exotic destinations and enjoying the latest and greatest products made by man.

The extreme disconnect within this framework is the fact that the working class's wages do not increase when profits increase. The wages of workers are considered a product on the free market and are based on the amount of employees that are looking for work. The lesser employees there are that are looking for work, the higher wages will grow. The more workers looking for work the less demand there is for labor and therefore the price of labor goes down. The incentive of the laborer is not increased as profits grow for the company. The ownership and management continually benefit directly from the increase in profits. Their goal then is to increase work productivity and enjoy more profits and more luxuries while keeping wages stagnant or even decreasing labor spending. Karl Marx saw this trend in capitalism and industrialism the way it had been invented in the last 300 years. He believed this model of economics and society to be unsustainable and actually it will lead to a working class rebellion against the elite ruling class. He saw capitalism as an initial state of an advancing society. It is the result of the ingenuity and differences among humans. Humans with varying natural ability will form trades and ways of producing food, clothing and housing. This creates the need for trade among those who produce various goods and services and naturally funds the concept of capitalism. This is the natural progression from a hunter-gatherer society to a founding of an industrial state filled with trade.

This to Karl Marx was the natural state of human progression. The next step in human progression to Marx is the exploitation of the working class which happens as a result of the fact that as trades and technologies develop there are groups of people who invent these advents. These people may feel like they are owed something for their creation. This has to do with self-preservation. They might begin to have a skewed outlook on what their idea of happiness is. As they receive, the benefit of material items can substitute the love for material things for the natural state of happiness. When you combine the void that is filled with material items by a person who already holds the keys to production of a certain good or commodity you get someone or an organization that can use the position of power that comes with owning facets of production to exploit others to gain immense material wealth. The individuals and the organization that are in search of wealth coerce and manipulate to make their organization suit their desire for material wealth and things. This is an unnecessary and a painful period in human history where those who own the keys to production use them for their own personal benefit and not for the benefit of humanity. Before industrialization this could not happen as individuals did not control large portions of humans by employment.

This to Marx is why certain things can happen under industrialism that is impossible under a more individually based hunter-gatherer society. This is why he comments that it is the natural progression of human society to undergo a period of selfishness when humans start to take advantage of the goods and services provided by cooperative labor. The selfishness that humans display out of a mistake in the idea of self-preservation under industrialism is able to affect millions of people under the state of economics we experience. This brings Marx to the next step in human societal evolution which is the dissolution of the current societal and economic trends by the masses of workers. The selfishness that elite in corporations and management exhibit feeds into a mistake in self-preservation which is attaining all the material items possible while ignoring human relationships. It also without their knowing causes suffering of all of those underneath their influence. The weight of the decisions of elite in the corporations is immense considering the scope of many modern corporations.

The mistake in self-preservation can lead to the exploitation of workers which can result in lives filled with toiling labor and no leisurely time but can also result in unemployment which leads to homelessness, starvation and many other atrocities. It also can lead to a global economic crisis which we experience today. The combined selfishness that corporations can exhibit could lead to a

triangular system that filters all the worlds'
wealth into a few elite hands. This can cause
major problems with global unemployment and
global uprisings from masses who feel like
they are being exploited. This is a familiar
advent to which is occurring in front of our
eyes. The selfishness of corporations who
institute policies which attempt to create the
most efficient operations that maximize
profits cause many issues that are relevant to
the modern economic and political crisis. The
inequality of humans under industrialism is
then the result of individuals who have skewed
ideas of self-preservation implementing
policies and actions onto masses that work for
them as a result of a feeling of ownership of
a company.

Karl Marx was the biggest champion for
those who were being exploited by this system.
He called for the unionization of all workers
and the displacement of those who implemented
policies that exploited the masses. The
workers should then organize themselves into a
democratic work force. Instead of the elite
profiting off the success of the company all
of those who labor will equally profit off of
the success of the company. This does two
things; it eliminates strict social class
divisions between the elite and the masses and
it also gives incentive for workers to
contribute to the organization as they receive
the benefits of the work they provide. This
step in human economic evolution is what
occurs after the initial state of
industrialization. The domestication so to say
of cooperative economic production is the next
phase then the exploitation of workers by

those who feel they are entitled to mass wealth when leading certain companies.

The extent to which we see Karl Marx's theory play out today is an important and very relevant question. There are natural things that can affect businesses such as the availability of resources which are important for the industry such as the amount of metal that can be mined. Other resources such as plants like cotton which supplies the textile industry are subject to uncontrollable factors such as the weather. The things that can be controlled in industrialism are the amount and the quality of products being produced along with the parameters under which these things are produced. Industrialism and cooperative labor give humans the material things that are not available in nature. It improves the quality of living as a result of the material items making life easier. The goal of industrialism and cooperative labor is to improve the quality of life for humans. As Marx said the owners and management may high jack this concept and keep the benefits of labor and production only for themselves. They do this unknowingly as they simply are pursuing wealth for themselves and they inadvertently keep down those below them from their business policies. Under this mode of society industrialism can take a turn from being a positive for humanity and a way of improving the quality of life to a way of decreasing the value of life and the overall happiness of humans. Under a hunter-gatherer society work may amount to 25 hours a week and the rest is to be enjoyed with family, friends and leisurely time. A society who is under industrialism but exhibits mass exploitation for the wealth of the few may have wealthy who reap all the benefits of mass cooperative labor and masses that might have no other means of life besides tedious labor and sleep. They also will undergo psychological torment at work as there is a constant barrage from management to complete work faster and more efficiently. Under this state the masses can become very depressed and very desperate. This is the mentality Marx saw from the people during his life. He saw the next step in human society is to rid the world of the negatives of industrialization and so to say domesticate the world.

These variables can be controlled in business and society. It is the responsibility of the masses to assure the best outcomes from the cooperative labor and society we all enter into. These variables can be controlled and should be to allow for the best possible experience on earth. The inequality among humans in a very small way is due to natural differences among humans that occur from hereditary genes and the differences among desire amongst people. Some may desire to be the best while others are just in it for the fun. A major contributor to the inequality among men in the modern industrial complex is the ability for men to own and control means of production and use it for their own selfish desire rather than the good of all men and women. This is what Marx appeals is for a movement by the masses to equalize social classes and drive industry for the benefit of all humans rather than those who own and control industry. This will advance the standard of living for all humans and not just the few. It also put industrialization and

cooperative labor in its proper context which
is to improve the conditions of life on earth.

The World in Our Hands

Adam M. Yeoman

The American Way

The United States political and economic system is very unique to the world. Our culture is also very distinct and unique. To best describe our economic and political system you only have to look at the philosophy of Adam Smith and John Locke. The best way of describing the uniqueness of America is the extreme emphasis on individualism. This emphasis on individualism is both what makes America great and what will ultimately lead to our decline. It is the way that this trend exhibits itself which determines the outcomes we experience as a nation. Our emphasis on individualism in economics has brought us prosperity for those who have access to wealth. It has allowed for the extreme variety of products and services we have and for the variety of people with varying cultures who live in our country. In extreme cases however, this individualism has contributed to the selfishness that has brought our country and other countries into an economic crisis.

The theory of John Locke and Adam Smith predicate in some way the predisposition for a society to turn to an extreme form of individualism that can lead to economic collapse. The sustainability of capitalism is the question that needs to be answered. In America we practice capitalism with a ruthless approach. Business is business and contains no moral ground. Layoffs and the treatment of employees are simply decisions of equity and labor capital. The separation of any moral ground in the American business is what makes American business both efficient and immorally comprehensible at the same time. What the difference between American economic practice and most of the rest of the world is the end motive for producing goods and services. In America the single motive for production and the providing of services is a personal profit motive by the ownership and management of a company. Under this motive the only real purpose of a company to ownership is to continue receiving money from customers. It is not to create a better product for people or to give a job to someone who needs it. The way business is engineered in the United States, there is no moral implication. This in many ways is what leads to such an individualistic and somewhat selfish culture among Americans. This individualism taken to such an extreme state has also created a very isolated and materially focused culture. Most other countries in the world have a feeling of unity with those around them and in their society. This creates a more cooperative effort in economics and society and has some moral implication to the business that is done in their country or abroad. This individualism has brought us some advances that are uniquely American and are a highlight of our civilization globally but it also has led us into our current economic decline.

The way in which the United States was founded has a lot to do with this individual culture and economic practice. The United States had no modern infrastructure to build on or use at first colonization. After many temporary settlements in the New World the first permanent settlements in the North and South attributed to this individual sentiment that we experience today. In the North the pilgrims and puritans immigrated as wealthy aristocratic religious families. These families were not used to doing their own work such as cooking food and various chores. They had employees that did most of their normal labor for them. When they immigrated they expected the lower class individuals who came over to resume taking care of their needs as they had experienced in their aristocratic positions in Europe. This was one form of thought that was intensely magnified when the New World was founded, as the split was already there between aristocrats and laborers. There was also tons of labor to be completed to successfully colonize the New World. It magnified the pressure that was put on laborers to complete tasks that were asked of by the aristocratic class. The laborers completed this labor as it was the only means of being paid. This created a very strict management style with laborers as the aristocrats were stressed from not having the luxuries they had in the old world. The aristocrats began to look out only for themselves as individuals as they struggled to live in a world cut off from the rest of the world until regular trade and travel to the New World began.

In the South the same sort of trend occurred with one variable being the growing of cash crops such as tobacco and cotton to sell back to Europe and bring trade goods to the new world. In the South in early colonization the infrastructure of villages was built in the same manner as the North but with the cash crops the South was able to run plantations that would allow for trade and the movement of goods back and forth from the old world to the new. The mentality that persisted in the South as regards to social organization was somewhat similar to a drug cartel of today. The leaders of these plantations demanded tremendous results from the workers. A rugged sense of individualism developed both in the North and the South as settlers were taken away from the benefits they had in a cooperative society that provided for their needs in Europe. The individual nature of New World people came as a necessity. Not having the benefits of society as described by Rousseau led humans to become adapted to individualism in a sense. In Europe the benefits of thousands of years of society were available for humans. In the New World there were only Native cities that the settlers did not use to their advantage. This made individuals who colonized America rely on themselves and experience stress and hardship trying to survive in an undeveloped environment. The experiences that arose out of this hard labor and stress influenced many of

the ideas that were founded in America. These
ideas arose out of the struggles of living in
this new continent but have maintained even
when this New World has been domesticated and
industrialized to the point that we do not
experience the same struggles early Americans
did. It is understandable that certain ideas
developed under original colonization but is
questionable whether some of the ideas and
measures that were put into place in early
America are the right ideas and measures for
modern industrialized America. This is
especially concerning when countries such as
France have rewritten their government and
economic principles almost every century. We
have kept the same economic and political
measures since the founding of our nation
which were reasoned out of a completely
different world which was based on
individualism as a necessity and not a theory.
I am not saying all American political
economic theory is irrelevant it is just
certain characteristics of the theories and
practice are relevant to a completely
different time period and are being forced
onto a completely different society. This
makes some of the American theory and practice
obsolete for all intensive purposes.

II.
    The theorists who influenced early American
and the creation of our government and
economic system cater to this concept of
individualism and material ownership. The main
theorist who inspired American political
theory was John Locke. Most remember what they
learned in high school about the rights to
private property as prescribed by John Locke.
John Locke covered the natural rights of man

as it pertains to freedom. The freedom from over extensive royal rule and the right to one's own private property are the major points made by Locke.

The concept of possession being nine tenths of the law came with Locke. He reasoned that man was capable of deciding what is good for him and is inherently a rational being. He wrote his treatise as a reaction to the monarchial rule that was experienced throughout Europe during his life and in history. He saw the ability of Monarchial governments to seize people's property for the state and also institute laws and regulations that overstepped into what Locke calls parental laws. These laws overstep the freedom of the individual to make decisions pertaining to him or herself. The main point he draws is that laws should protect actions that may harm others as a result of the action but should have no jurisdiction in laws that pertain solely to the treatment of one's self. The use of John Locke's theory was used to justify the weakening of monarchies in Europe and the implementation of a parliamentary democracy. In the United States when our Constitution was written it was used to influence the creation of a bill of rights so that the power would end up residing in the individual rather than the government or monarchy. It also created the notion of private property and very strict laws on stealing and trespassing. He is also quoted any time a law comes to pass which seems to restrict the individual from doing something that may harm him but not others. The argument is that man is his own free being and has this natural right bestowed on him by our creator. We should then be able to make choices that affect ourselves even if it is an ultimately negative choice.

The theories of John Locke and the focus on the individual have taken on a life of its own in America. The extreme extent in which we cater to the individual has allowed for some to manipulate the ideas of John Locke to suit their own selfish individual needs. The biggest modern use of John Locke is to justify the elimination of social welfare benefits. Those in wealthy privileged positions attest that the government funding of the poor is a government overreach and is also a way of unjustly taking property. Locke however, only meant that government should be limited of doing such things as enforcing religion or a certain culture and drug policy. He did not have any problem with government helping its exploited and poor citizens he just wanted the government to maintain that individuals ultimately have sovereignty over themselves. John Locke's theory of the individual maintaining sovereignty is embedded in our legal system and in the creation of our political system.

III.

The political system in the United States was modeled after the tripartite parliament found in Britain. This is the system of a ruler or president and then a higher parliament or Senate and a lower parliament representing districts or the House of Representatives in our case. This divides the powers of government into three modes of power that become decreasingly less influential as you go down the line. The president maintains the most power followed by the Senate and then in the House of Representatives. This is modeled after the economic system that perpetuated itself in Europe which displayed the triangular system of the Aristocrats followed by ownership and management and then the peasants. The president is then the manifestation of the Aristocracy into government power while the Senate is a representation of those who are closer to the aristocracy while the masses of peasants are represented in the lower house.

Our political system is designed to fit a class system that comes with industrialism. It is no wonder that it seems the outcomes of government policy only seem to suit those who already have access to the aristocracy. It is a government that was created to fit the economic system that developed under the industrial boom in Europe. Previously in Britain there was no real representational form of government. It was simply rule by royals who were of noble birth. The invention of a representative democracy started in Britain and with the succession of the United States it was implemented onto the new country. This is the United States political system. It is an answer to the issues of representation that result when industry creates new aristocracy. This created the need for representation of the new elite which gave rise to the creation of the parliament. This idea was used to form the United States government. By design the governmental system that we use in America was designed to represent the needs of industrial corporations. The difference between the government and system of the United States and Great Britain is the implementation of John

Locke's theory of the individual. In Great Britain the needs of industrial representation were implemented but they were not willing to let go of the Monarchial system that has lasted for hundreds if not thousands of years. We have a mix of the representational form of government in Europe that was a response to industrialization and the theories of John Locke which attempt to put power in the individual and rid the world of hereditary rule but rather democratically elected rule.

The representational form of government allows for the election of representatives from local districts so that the national government comprises of the opinions and issues of the entire country and not just certain locations. The ability for a person to be elected in a region is tied heavily to the connections and prior experience with powerful and wealthy people in the region. In Britain this was most certainly the case as the elected officials were basically representatives of the regional corporations. The system in the United States was modeled after this so it is no wonder why the same trend seems to occur for elected officials here. When a candidate seeks to run for government in the United States he or she must raise enough money to portray their policy platform to the public. This is done by seeking donations from normal citizens and receiving lobbying money from local corporations that seek to extend their influence into national affairs. Recently the Supreme Court upended a limit on the donations that candidates can receive from corporations so this aspect of fundraising is a major player in today's elections.

In many ways you can see that the modern electoral system breeds representation from corporations and not from individuals. This is in many ways because the system was originally built as a response to industrialism. There have been other societies in the past that practiced democracy more so for the sake of practicing it as a moral implication. Athens, Greece, and France were extreme models of pure democracy that have been tried. Our specific system for all intensive purposes is just the political answer to the advent of industrialization, corporatism and individualism. It would make perfect sense under our current system that those who have money by becoming influential in industrialism would be able to have more of a say then the average working individual. This is because the system is designed as an extension of corporatism onto the political landscape. In many ways under industrialism previous notions of political problems have been replaced by the issues that are faced by corporations in a modern world. Economics has replaced the power void that used to be fulfilled by monarchs and military leaders.

IV.

Our country is unique because we have thousands of power bases in various powerful corporations around the country. These power bases exert control over local populations and in some ways contain and exert more control and influence than the national government and local political institutions. We are a series of corporations that exert influence on local and national affairs. These companies extend their influence by lobbying and supporting politicians who will represent their interests

in Government. In the early 19th century the
intertwinement of Government and corporations
was so thick that the military was used in
many instances to secure off shore production
areas for many corporations. Entire countries
were taken over by the United States military
for the use of corporations such as fruit
companies and many others. Many in South
America and other areas of the world were
killed in cold blood so that we could have
control over fruit.

The best way to describe America is that it
is a nation of corporatism. Corporations are a
collection of individuals who seek to grow and
extend their influence and power.
Individualism is valued as many of the tactics
exhibited value in those who individually
perform relative to others and with this
individual success they are promoted to a new
class of employee. The symbols of these
corporations are not so much the common brand
or the product but in many ways are the CEO's.
They are individual representations of masses
of people who make up a corporation. Again,
the focus is completely on the individual who
represents and leads the corporation and not
the collection of people who really make the
company run. The celebration of the individual
is everywhere in society. Individuals on
sports teams define the team more so than the
collective organization. Actors define movies
more so than the general quality of the movie.
I am not saying any of these trends are
completely wrong or are bad but is an example
of the extreme individualism we as Americans
value. In many other countries they exhibit
more of cooperative notion in things such as
sports, movies and corporations. In sports the

team is defined by the overall success the
team has and movies are judged by the overall
story while companies value overall
performance and the masses of employees who
make it run rather than the leaders. The
individualism we display is not all bad as
individuals strive to be the best they can be
for themselves and lead to tremendous
achievements. We as a country have produced
many of the top athletes, actors and symbolic
products around the world.

This has to do with the tremendous spirit
individuals have in rising above the
limitations that seem to be set for us. It
also has to do with the previous economic
prosperity in which allows for the funding of
athletes, actors and corporations. The
individualism we display goes back to the
scattered immigration of the United States and
the economic culture we displayed. The concept
of entrepreneurship and the American dream of
being independent, owning your own home and
property became the ideal American life. In
other countries simply having the necessities
of survival and a healthy family and social
network of friends is more so what people
strive to achieve. We have enjoyed the
individual wealth and property that is unique
to American and it has been embedded in our
culture and tradition. This has been embedded
in many areas of American life such as the way
we educate our children, our legal, economic
and political systems. The intense
individualism leads to very prideful world
view. This arises out of the indoctrination we
teach our kids about winning and being the
best. We believe and act as though we are the
best and the only right way of doing things.

This leads to a very confident and assured public. We continue to become better as individuals. The only negative is the lacking of the ability to empathize with others' way of life and the struggles they might go through.

The individualism that is displayed in America can make it hard to empathize with others' struggles as you are not concerned with the collective good but only your individual success. This has led to the struggles that many experience in America. With complete individualism in economics and politics comes competition; and with competition there becomes winners and losers. When there are winners and losers in economics there becomes a very stratified society. This individualism is a good thing for self confidence and individual great achievements but when combined with an economic system that produces winners and losers it can put strain on the general welfare of all in society. The individualism we display is both what makes our nation great and at the same time is what is leading to our economic collapse. Our economic and political system which is built on corporations who compete with other corporations only feed into the mentality of complete individualism. Individual success should not be punished when it is in the best interests of all. The problem lies when individuals succeed at something that may hold down thousands of others. The way in which individuals succeed must be coupled with the general welfare of the United States. In other countries if an individual were to rise up and succeed but either bankrupt their corporation or lead to a loss for their sports team they would not be celebrated. They would in actuality be looked down on even worse than if they simply tried their best and lost as an organization or team as a whole. The individualism at once creates the great symbols of our society but also give us the reputation as an indoctrinated and cruel country that does not help out any one less fortunate.

The differences that arise from this idea of individualism lend itself in every area of American life. For instance in foreign work places the idea of being fired is not really prevalent. If you are unable to perform a certain task within the company you will simply be demoted to a position that suits your skills better. It is the cooperative effort of the company that counts and not individual efforts. Economics is than less selfish and more cooperative even in other capitalist countries. They maintain the benefits of capitalism but maintain a certain communal effort in industry that keeps things working for the benefit of the country as a whole and not individuals alone. This leads to the creation of many policies within American companies and organizations that spur competition among people within a company and create somewhat of a hostile work environment. Whereas in other countries people are a member of a team and work together to achieve, in America we are individuals who struggle to come out on top within a company and hope that we are not going to be fired. This does many things such as tremendously raise the stress that people experience in the workplace while creating tremendous uncertainty for the future. This on a micro level can lower employee morale, increase employee confrontation and decrease cooperation.

   On a macro level it can actually stunt the growth of a national economy, lead to tremendous unemployment, increase the crime rate and tear down the general morale of the country. This occurs because of the nature of capitalism and private business. When there is competition between businesses and people in the United States over time certain people and businesses develop monopolies on certain industries. These monopolies seek to take out any other competition and use their resources to do so. They have a tremendous advantage of resources including capital and the best lawyers money can buy. They attempt to buy or dismantle any competing corporations. The smaller business is subject to less resources and avenues to protect themselves and is eventually squashed from the pressure put on them by monopolies. The reason businesses seek to become a monopoly is because of the competition that is inherent in our economy. They want to win and be the best by becoming rich. To become rich they need to corner the market on a certain product or service so they can benefit. This individualistic idea of success is different in America than it is in most places around the world. Although, people around the world strive to be as prosperous as they can honor and appreciation from people in society is in some ways more important than attaining individual wealth. Our society looks up to those who become extravagantly rich and this psychologically influences people to seek out this ideal to be looked up to. In many ways it is not being filthy rich but to attain a position of respect and admiration in society that is strived for. In other areas of the world to gain admiration from your peers you must do something of value to the society as a whole. If you were to become extravagantly wealthy from selling a valued company in the community you would be demonized rather than celebrated for your rich status. The difference is that in other areas of the world success is determined by the standards of the society as a whole rather than the individual.

V.

    In America we value individualism and look at the success of the individual over what that success meant to the society as a whole. Someone like Donald Trump is valued for his monopoly on the hotel and real estate industry. Donald Trump has a reputation for poor employee treatment and ripping off people in business dealings. He also runs a show that basically makes many people compete for a certain job and ruthlessly fire people at a moment's whim. In America he is considered an icon because of his immense wealth and property ownership. In other countries he would be thought of as a selfish mogul who is corrupting the hotel and real estate industry while ruining many employees' lives. They would see the impact that he has on society and not the individual implications of his wealth. In America we ignore the societal impact and look at the individual implications which are the fact that he got rich and enjoys material things that most of us cannot have. When others visit our country they see people's names on things such pillows, towels and soap and wonder why in the world people would do something like that. They see these items as something that we have as a benefit of society and not because an individual like Donald Trump owns the trump towers and chooses to represent his name on all of the items that are within his hotel. These differences in perception of success in society, and the proper way of acting once attaining economic power make two very different societies.

The United States is defined by the unique way in which our economic power is used. We sparked mass industrialization in the world and have spread our knowledge and skills of mass production. Other countries have taken our model and have run with it to develop areas of the world that were previously living under classical conditions. We are very similar to the rest of the world in that we influenced how the world operates under mass industrialism. The difference lies in the way in which we use industrialism as a tool for society. We use it as a tool for individuals to rise above the collective and become wealthy and independent. Other areas of the world use industrialism and mass production to raise the general standard of living for all in society. Industrialism is a tool in which the society can help stop the struggle that comes with classical society and lacking material conveniences that create an easier life. Industrialism is a way in which humanity can change our surroundings and paint onto the world a landscape of our design. It is how we use this new advent of industrialization that creates the world we live in. We can use it for the common good of all or for individuals to become powerful and rule over the rest of society. If we use industrialization as a tool to exploit and conquer, the world will look much like our countries and the world's early industrial history which was plagued with suffering and death from the world wars. On the other side we could use industrialization to stop suffering and create a better and happier life for our children in the future.

Our country has a mixed history of its use of industrialism. We have accomplished great things such as sending man into space and giving the world things such as the telephone and the internet. We have also had a Great Depression which impoverished millions and millions of Americans. We did not do much to help with the suffering as we felt intervention in economics to be a blasphemy. We have also launched military expeditions against countries who have neither the infrastructure nor military industrialization to properly defend them-selves. We have sold deadly weapons to non-developed countries where factions now have the ability to kill in mass. We have jailed millions of Americans for non violent crimes that go against the cultural norms of society. Our military has accomplished good things in the world such as help stop the rise of Nazi Germany and attempt to stop genocide in the former Yugoslavia. But with industrialism comes a whole new set of problems for the world. Before the ability to mass produce modern war weapons, countries and armies were limited to the amount of destruction that could be done to the world. A classical army could invade a city with bows, arrows and swords but could not simply fire artillery and drop bombs from miles away. In the modern era conflicts can exponentially blow up into something so heinous that when told in history it is almost thought of as impossible or unrealistic but it has already happened on this planet we all share. We have been the only country to use the force of nuclear weapons on civilians. We incinerated two entire Japanese cities filled with men, women and children. Instantly hundreds of thousands of people were killed. The weight and effect of our actions under modern industrialism are exponentially increased and with this power comes much greater responsibility. This great responsibility we carry with industrialism is in many ways the story of America. We have harnessed great technologies and have built a uniquely modern civilization but struggle to deal with all of the new challenges that come with this advent.

This struggle defines America and the rest of the world. We struggle as Americans to succeed as individuals in a mass society. This struggle is displayed in our modern economic climate where millions are unemployed and hope to carve out a spot for themselves in society. On a macro level our government and administration struggles to help run a society in which all people need employment in the industrial complex to have access to the support system of humanity. On a micro level we hope and fight for the remaining jobs that can give us access to the goods and services we need to survive. The hard part about industrialism is that humans are taken away from the support system of nature and are then reliant on the support system of society. In America we are expected to be individuals in industrialism without the support of society so in many ways we only deal with the hard parts of industrialism and lose out on the

benefits of being in a cooperative society.
Just as the responsibility increases with the
new versions of war weapons the same goes for
the economy. The greater our economy is the
more spread out and alienated people can
become. They are completely pulled away from
the support system of nature and are reliant
only on the fact that those around them in
society will continue to operate and bring the
goods and services to their obscure location.
The responsibility we carry as humans has
increased as we develop and with this
responsibility comes a greater need for
cooperation and solidarity among humans so
that we can all prosper on this earth.

VI.

In America today we struggle to balance
industrialism and capitalism with the needs of
all in our society. Our political landscape is
a fight between those who control and own
industry and business and the masses of
people. This is split between the Democrats
who represent the masses of people and the
Republicans who represent individual business
interests and those who seek to make
Christianity more intertwined in our country.
The Republicans who represent individual
business interests seek to make it impossible
for anyone including government to interfere
in their ability to make a huge profit from
their business. They believe America to be a
place in which individuals can pursue their
own interests and attain mass wealth. They
want to protect this way of life and to create
regulations and laws favoring workers that
would undermine their ability to do business
the way they have been in which has led to
their immense wealth. This way of life has in

some ways led to the economic collapse. They do not care about the macro effects they cause because of the ideology that America is a nation of individuals and we each are responsible for our own fate. The fact is that the selfishness and the individualism that is displayed by business owners and managers leads to an economic downturn when certain actions are taken to pursue profits. These actions include the quest for cheaper operating costs to increase profits, lowering the wages and benefits of current employees, engineering the market areas to keep prices high and failing to use profits to reinvest in the company. All of these trends contract economic growth and handicap the ability for the economy to expand in the future. The quest for cheaper operating costs lead to the minimization of human involvement in labor. Two ways that a company can do this is one; to make current employees more efficient and fire the remaining ones and two; to automate labor with machinery that eliminates the need for employees in the first place. Another way to reduce costs is to simply lower current employee's wages and benefits. This puts more money into the pockets of ownership and management which in turn increases profits.

The textbook for growth in capitalism is the use of profits to expand and grow a business. If a company is seeking profits for themselves as individuals they would see no reason to invest in their business. The only reason they would invest in their business would be the hope of turning a higher rate of profit in the future. These types of investments as I mentioned eliminate jobs and decrease wages and benefits. All of these actions increase the living standard and wealth of individuals who own and control business. They however decrease the amount of jobs available for the masses and lower the general wages of workers. As you can see what increases the wealth of these individuals actually shrinks the economy and a macro scale.

In capitalism the individual business only succeeds when they have a reliable customer base in which they can sell their services to and receive a profit. When the whole system of our nation operates under the same rules of capitalism and individuals seek to maximize profit this means that what one business does is going to affect the consumer base of another. If every business seeks to eliminate labor costs by performing the actions I mentioned this means that a significant portion of America will go through a decrease in wages or a complete loss of income. This creates a circular effect that in essence can bring the national economy to its knees and completely halt any growth and start a sharp contraction in economic output. This happens because the initial individual measures of companies to increase profits by decreasing the wages of workers or simply laying off employees to increase personal profit.

At the same time one business does this every other company figures out that this might increase their wealth too. Over time the amount of Americans with income that they can use towards purchasing goods and services decrease. Once, when these people had income and a job they would purchase more clothing and food which would support businesses in their area. Once every business begins to eliminate employees and lower others wages for personal profit they single handedly take out the consumer base that allowed for the success of their business in the first place. A circular effect occurs in which companies see an initial increase in profits from decreasing labor costs but then experience a decrease in sales. This decrease in sales causes them to lay off more employees and lower the wages of existing workers. This then decreases the consumer base even more and eventually the company does not have enough sales to even operate and goes out of business. This circular effect has hit our economy and has led to a recession in which the masses suffer and businesses become desperate as they cannot figure out why they experience such a decrease in success. This all happened as a result of the idea that individuals should look out for themselves and deserve complete control over their company.

With this individual control of their company they do not realize they are not only harming masses of people but are handicapping their business from being successful in the future as there will be no one who can spare money to purchase the product or service they sell. These businesses that have become desperate and represent the support base for the Republican Party who seeks to influence policy to favor their business even more so they can become profitable again. Their ideas include things such as tax breaks for their business operations and the further ability for companies to lower wages and eliminate mandatory benefits for employees. They want further funding for the ability to off shore labor for even cheaper operating costs. The elimination of social welfare programs to them would decrease their tax rate and contribute to the profits that they see. This part seeks to represent businesses who are desperate and cannot understand why they are not experiencing the success they have had in the past. Unrenowned to them all of these policies would actually take more money away from consumers and lead to a decrease in sales even more so than they already have experienced.

VII.

On the other hand of political representation you have the Democrat party who seeks to represent the masses and get the economy moving again by using government spending as a way of stimulating economic growth. The Democrat party sees some of the economic and political trends that are occurring because of the selfishness and individualism that is displayed by American corporations. They see how actions taken by American corporations are harming the general good of society and seek to represent those who have been harmed. The people who have been harmed are those in society who have no ties to ownership in corporations and rely on being an employee as the primary way of providing for themselves and their family. The amounts of people who rely on this mode of living substantially outweigh those who reap huge profits from the ownership of business. This has allowed for the election of an administration who seeks to represent the large portion of society who is paid by labor and not for the shear fact that they own a mode of production or service. These citizens lobby for fair treatment in the work place and access to the basic services that are required to live in our modern world. They seek the ability to provide housing for themselves and their children without undue harassment from banks, they seek to be paid the amount of money that their labor is worth to society and not what it is valued on a labor market that is set up by those who benefit from lowering labor costs, they wish to provide themselves and their children food in which will nourish rather than cause problems such as high cholesterol and obesity among adults and children. All of these things and more would cause a loss of wealth and power to many who own and control business.

The two parties carry completely conflicting ideals and come to a disagreement on almost every major issue that affects our country. The reason being is that what benefits the masses and poor actually loses money and power for those who hold power and wealth currently. The interest of the wealthy and those who control and own business conflicts with what is good and needed for the masses. When the masses of people lobby for their best interest in the work place and society it actually threatens the perceived livelihood of those in power. If wages were increased for workers, vacation time was available, employees participated in elite decisions of company operations, and management was dissolved to allow employees to govern themselves; those who own and control business would lose the ability to become extravagantly wealthy. They would end up at the same social status as the rest of us. Their stranglehold on the control of

information, religion and the economy would
diminish.

Many in this social class understand this
is the case. Others simply were born into this
class and are indoctrinated with the ideas
that others who work for them are lazy and the
only way to keep them on the right track in
their lives is to instill hard work ethics and
the Christian religion onto them for their own
good. We have a complete separation of a
privileged aristocracy and the masses. Those
from the privileged aristocracy have their own
customs, culture and morals that are a direct
result of their experiences in life. It is
completely separate from the struggle the
average person from the masses goes through in
their life. Neither the wealthy business class
nor the masses seem to identify with the other
and it has caused the immense divide in
American politics we see today. The issues
that the masses face are serious and affect
such important things that it is imperative we
as a nation resolve the issues at hand.
Globally people suffer from the lack of basic
needs such as nourishment, housing and proper
clothing.

VIII.
    In our modern world the United States is
seeing these same issues. The masses of
workers who are affected by the recession are
experiencing homelessness, malnutrition and a
lack of proper cold weather clothing. They
also lose hope for the future as they feel it
is almost impossible to find a job especially
when you have been unemployed for some time.
The loss of hope and the humiliation from
going from a contributor to society and all of

a sudden laid off and thrown into poverty is
the general story for millions of Americans
through this recession. In other areas of the
world people simply do not have the material
resources to live the lifestyle we do. I am
not downplaying these people's struggles at
all but the fact is, is that these human
societies can survive without the material
resources as they are near areas in which they
can hunt, gather and live more so off of the
land. There is still suffering when nature
does not provide what the people need. In
America we live in such urban environments
that when humans are cut off from the supply
of the economy there is absolutely no way they
can live off of natural resources. After
unemployment runs out for many Americans they
are forced onto the street with no means in
which to provide for themselves or their
children. This is the struggle that many
Americans face or fear that they will face if
something is not done to change the way
employees are treated in American companies.

   This is in stark contrast to what people
who own and control business experience during
a recession. This sector of America may see a
drop in their stock value and lose customers
but still make enough money to keep the same
lifestyle they have been living for some time.
They might not be able to afford the vacation
home they were looking at in Florida or buy
their son or daughter a top of the line sports
car. We as Americans have a moral obligation
to stop people from needlessly suffering on
our own soil. We also have an international
obligation to do what we can to stop needless
suffering globally. Our modern society can
produce the goods and services that can stop

suffering and have all the tools to create a better world.

Currently, however, we do not use our success and ability to do well for others; but focus only on the success of individuals who come out on top in society. It seems as our national culture is that humans are not being helped, but being given the tools so they themselves can succeed and become an individual. This is so embedded in our culture that it is thought of as almost a crime to give someone something they did not earn even if they were in desperate need. The extreme extent to which we have used this idea has caused many people who ordinarily could have been helped but were denied because of our national culture were abandoned. There is nothing wrong with providing someone with a job that ensures that they can earn the things they need to provide for their children. The idea that giving someone tools to succeed such as a job does work.

The national situation we face economically does not allow for this version of help to happen. There are upwards of 40 million unemployed or underemployed workers searching for work. The amount of jobs that are created each month is staggeringly low. There is absolutely no way that even a portion of these people can be provided help by being given a job with the current way things are operated. The reason why there is a lack of jobs has to do with the individualism and selfishness displayed by American companies. This is where the clash happens between the two parties in America. The only way the people suffering in America are going to be helped is to give them the things they need for survival such as food, clothing and shelter. We have to use the combined prosperity of those in America to help the least among us until we can provide the tools for them to succeed independently. The stance of the Democrat party is to provide these things through government programs and incentives for businesses to help these suffering people. The Republican Party sees free help given to these people as an invasion of their rights and that the people suffering must simply pull themselves up from the situation they are under. This is nearly impossible as the amount of jobs available make certain that each job contains hundreds if not thousands of applicants. Only one is chosen for the position and hundreds are left in their current struggle.

Republicans cannot see this fact and refuse to help those who experience hardships because of the ideology that has been imprinted on America since its founding. It is almost thought of as insane when other countries look at how America is handling our situation. Most humans are taught as a child that sharing and helping others is an inherently moral value. In America there is such a stigma that goes with providing people free goods and services that the ideology trumps the inherent nature of humans to help others. Our political landscape is filled with those who fight for the masses of people who need help and those who hold onto the indoctrination that has permeated because of the intense individualism in the United States.

IX.

This difference between the two sectors of American society becomes apparent in most of America's political and legal institutions. Depending on the area of the country certain trends take a hold of the various institutions. In some areas various criminal courts and law enforcement agencies take a one sided stance on how to handle the citizens under their jurisdiction. Some identify with the business owning class and perpetuate the control that business exerts on the population as well as laws that perpetuate American religious values. In these areas for instance the way that courts follow legal codes strongly leans towards rulings that ultimately will favor business and those that seek to push religious values onto a population. Seemingly irrational laws and trends in court rulings occur because of this trend. Whatever the control group's views are is what is going to be represented onto their local legal and political system. As laid out in our country's founding, local states, cities, counties, and towns maintain certain autonomy in how they handle their political and legal issues. If the control group in the region makes a living off of either owning a business or heading a religious church or group they may seek to extend the influence they have in gearing the area's legal and political operations to suit their individual needs.

Certain areas of our country have such strict prosecution on any offense that is against a business's best interest that seemingly juvenile crimes end up carrying long term jail sentences and huge fines. These crimes include things such as petty larceny, minor drug offenses and the swift suing of anyone who owes any money to area businesses and etc. The crime of petty larceny should be prosecuted as stealing cannot be part of a healthy society, but the amount of time and punishment some receive in certain areas of the country rival the amount violent offenders receive. This is because of the lobbying and placement of the court system by business to protect their interests which is maintaining profit. Any loss of inventory directly decreases their ability to make a profit. They escalate the punishment for these crimes to scare off other potential shop lifters but many young men and women lose their young lives in prison for a minor offense. This is also true of minor drug offenses that involve non-addictive drugs such as Marijuana. The reason that minor drug offenses end up carrying punishment that exceeds many other more serious crimes is a direct result of the intertwinement of religious values with the local court and law enforcement systems. Again, the sentences become escalated as the courts attempt to scare others in society from using these drugs because of the ideological stance against the use of mind altering substances. This carries the unintended consequence of many young men and women having to live out very long jail sentence over something seemingly not criminal. All of these trends lead to the fact that the United States carries the highest percentage of citizens that are imprisoned in the world. This carries human rights issues and also puts tremendous strain on the legal and prison system. Many prisons become overcrowded and actually release violent offender's early on good behavior while some drug and theft offenders cannot be released as clauses on their sentences. Many court judgments that involve money and not jail time are also geared to favor those who own and control business.

Rental law can be seen as the most blatant example of this trend. During a lease if a person happens to be laid off from work or experiences a decrease in income there is absolutely no recourse for the renter to get out of the 12 month agreement. This means that a person becomes laid off and unemployment cannot cover rent they will be evicted because of not paying rent. Not only do they instantly become homeless they then are sued by a local court to pay the remaining balance on the twelve month lease. They may receive a court notice that the vehicle they worked so hard to pay off will be seized to pay off the balance on the apartment. This occurs and the apartment owners get the money for the lease and the tenants end up still being homeless. All the while the apartment owners get someone else in that apartment and start a new lease while receiving the money from the homeless tenant's car. This is blatantly an instance in which the control group implemented laws and customs that favor them. If this to were happen in some other area of the world where the court system sought justice the actions taken by the apartment owners would be seen as criminal and a violation of inherent rights of the renter. This is a border line human rights violation of international law.

Since the control group drew up the rules and customs of the area the victim is now seen as the perpetrator. The same trends that occur with rental law seem to play out in the home owning circle as the law blatantly favors the banks that provide mortgages. Many Americans are being told by financers that if they miss a few payments on their mortgage they can then refinance the mortgage to make it more affordable. Once the home owners follow their advice they are told that they cannot refinance and that they are now under foreclosure from missing the payments on their house. The banks carry the best lawyers money can buy and have already lobbied courts and lawmakers to draw up laws that favor their best interests. This is stacked up against a family who is already experiencing hardship and scrapes together just enough money to pay for a lawyer. The family never wins as the law code is set to provide no recourse for anyone to win against the bank. The only way to provide any relief is to catch the bank in a quagmire where they did not keep the proper paperwork to document their claim against you. This only delays the process and eventually most of these families with children end up thrown out on the streets. This has nothing to do with their lack of work ethic or laziness; it has everything to do with the whims that American corporations go on when laying off employees for increased personal profit. As you can see the control group in a society has much more resources and embedded influence that makes getting their way very easy. It seems to be almost impossible to fight against this group and win.

X.

   As local jurisdictions can display the trends of the business owning and religious classes so can the national political scene. The national political scene is under a

constant stream of lobbyists who seek to
influence the operations of our national
government. The banks, oil companies, and
other large corporations flex their economic
muscle by paying hefty dues to any congressmen
or women who will empathize with their issues.
The House of Representatives and the Senate
are constantly being bombarded with the issues
that large corporations seek to get across in
the national political order. Many of these
initiatives end up getting passed in congress.
The intertwinement of the control group in a
society and the policies of that society are
very embedded and prevalent. For most of
American history big business and our national
government were nearly one in the same as big
business paid the politicians who operated
government. In recent times we have seen one
of the first times that a president seeks to
run government for the masses of people and
not the control group. It is no wonder that
the president receives a constant barrage of
propaganda that seeks to regain control of
government by the people who have always been
in power. This clash of ideals defines
American life.

Currently we resemble more closely the
ideals of the Republican Party and those who
seek to make America a place to do business
and make profits. We are a nation of
businesses who see themselves as individuals
and should receive the rights that individuals
do. The ability for corporations to prosper
and make profits is the number one thing that
government and law provide for. These
corporations bring wealth and prosperity to
those who are in the in-crowd within the
company. Those who are not in the in-crowd may

experience very low wages, long hours, and very little job security. Our legal and political system is set up to represent those who are in the in-crowd of these corporations. They extend their influence the policies made by local and national government jurisdictions. They do with this with economic coercion. This is done by simply paying politicians and officials to represent their interests or by threatening to move the base of their operations which would lose jobs and stifle the economic success of the region it resides in. All of this means that corporations seek to be provided complete freedom to do whatever they please. What they want and what their motive is is to become wealthy and turn huge profits in each quarterly cycle of business. This does not take into consideration the treatment of their employees or customers. If they continue to make a profit the suffering of neither the employees nor the customers would have any bearing in their business decisions. This is why our country is filled with corporations who hold monopolies on industry and become very powerful in society. They can exert their control on local populations and get away with employee maltreatment because of the fact that they are one of the only employers in the area. There is a constant transfer of power from the average citizen to that of the corporation and their concern for profit. These companies provide our country a great service which is the production of the goods and services that we need to prosper as a nation. The thing that needs to be realized is that the way companies do business has much wider effects than most would think.

The management and ownership of companies feel as though they are succeeding and doing well if they are making a profit. What they do not take into account is the tremendous responsibility they have to society. The larger their business becomes and the more of a monopoly they become the more they will exponentially increases the responsibility they carry. With this responsibility they must act as a morally conscious entity. They hold the power to create success for everyone employed by them. They also hold the power to destroy the lives of those employed by them. The customers that use their product or service also count on the safety and reliability of their product or service to survive. If these companies fail in acting within a proper moral context they can cause tremendous unintended consequences to society as a whole.

The case of Detroit and the exporting of car manufacturing single handedly decimated a once great city and led to mass unemployment and suffering for Detroit. On a national scale millions have become unemployed at the whim of these corporations seeking more efficient operations. Families and their children have been left homeless and hungry. Our nation's international reputation had been damaged from the maltreatment of our nation's citizens. Millions of houses are being foreclosed as families experience sudden unemployment. Important companies who provide useful services and products are closing down as a result of the lack of spending from the high unemployment rate. The bottom line is that when these large companies take action it can have a very good effect on society or a very bad effect. If they choose to take action that affects America but is in their best interest and harms the rest of society, it can have devastating consequences to society. The larger the company and the more powerful they become the greater weight is placed on actions that they make. This is the story of our nation.

It is a conglomeration of large corporations who can either create our success or lead to our demise. We rely on the actions these companies take to determine our lives. They provide us with the goods and services we all need. On the side of the customer we hope that the things that we need will stay at a price that is affordable. On an employee side we hope we can maintain employment and not experience an overabundance of stress related to our job. In our lives the experience we have working with our companies and purchasing goods from other companies makes up a huge portion of the life we experience. We are so tied to the industrial world we experience. This industrial world defines the political and legal world. The power of companies to control outcomes in the world is at an all time high. It is not the will of the people that is being represented in our political and economic discourse but the will of those who seek to benefit from the extreme profits that a company can exploit. Our modern world is defined by the power bases that are corporations. We have no power bases that rest with the people or the world. Corporations are not a democracy. They are a dictatorship that is run by those who own them. This results in power bases being in the hands of a few wealthy people that make decisions that affect the rest of society for the good or bad. In order for our human society to progress we need a common voice in important decisions rather than those who own and control industry.

Adam M. Yeoman

The World We Live In

The life we experience in this world is unique in that we can shape and create the life we experience. We have the ability to make changes and adjust things in this world. It all depends on what we choose to do with our lives as individuals and as a collective species. Our current world is a landscape of our design. It reflects the actions and ideas we have all taken. It is a creation of our design and not some unseen force that creates suffering. We put ourselves in situations where we lead ourselves into negative circumstances which produce suffering. This world we live in is full of needless suffering and this suffering is a result of many things but is not inherent. These problems can be corrected. The struggle we face as humans is a result of the way in which we organize ourselves in society. The problems we create for ourselves can have ramifications beyond what one would think. The actions taken by individuals can create an expanded web of effect which influences how many in society experience their lives.

The web of connection that we have as humans has increased exponentially with the modern world and industrialization. The power we have to alter our modern day world seems almost something of magic to those who inhabited the world in the past. The power we have to affect the world gives us that much more responsibility to take action that is not only good for ourselves but takes into consideration the good of all of those who share this world. There is a fine balance between local and world affairs and to not focus on the ramifications of actions taken in the world would be very irresponsible and would border on immoral. With this said, many leaders in industry and politics do not consider the ramifications of their actions and do not use rationality as a guiding force for their decisions. The actions and policies they implement carry a wide array of consequences for many people in our country and around the world. We as the United States are one of the few industrialized nations of which do not carry a large social welfare system and the use of government to gear private industry in the direction best suited for society. The government in most other nations is used as a representation of the people in society to counter the power of private industry.

This dichotomy of relations between the government and industry allows for the people in society to help direct industry to suit the proper needs of the country and not just the individuals who control business. This helps the country make decisions that represent the good of all in society and not just those who stand to profit from industry. The hands-off approach to industry and economics has been the hallmark of the American industrialized society but it has led to economic prosperity for a few individuals while somewhat harming others. The actions that companies take can have exponential affects to the rest of society, they are not isolated entities. With our current system companies do not act with rationality, but rationality is defined by profit. When companies succeed according to their values they are successful and make profits and with this trend they do not fully understand the ramifications of any action that they take. This does not mean that corporations do not do any good as they provide a way for humans to shape our reality through creations of human ingenuity. These companies can do things that other human generations could only imagine in their science-fiction novels or dreams. The power that corporations have can be used to do so much good in the world and they can also use the economic power they have as leverage to coerce and garner unjustified wealth. Currently, companies do a mixture of good and bad in society. They provide products and services that are not known to any other human generation. On the other hand, they take irrational actions because of the motive of profit. The profit motive does not have a basis in rationality; while corporations provide us the modern world we experience they can also have a disruptive effect to the balance of society.

If corporations base their decisions and actions solely on the ability to make more profit there becomes an extreme disconnection between what is good for society and what is good for profit. The concept that businesses are for turning profit and making individuals wealthy is deeply embedded into our culture and society. This is where the idea comes from that states actions taken under business do not carry a moral value; business is business and is thought to be separate from normal life. The reality however is that business plays nearly the most important function in life and the decisions businesses make carry great responsibility and affect many people. When they make decisions that make money for the company they are praised by the people in their business network. They may be hated by those who were affected negatively by the decisions they made, but they do not consider this unless it affects the bottom line which is their profit. There is a complete lack of rationality in their decision making processes, the only rational they see is whether they will make more money on the business deal. This is because our country has geared economics and culture to celebrate those who can become wealthy through business. This is fine as long as the quest for profit is in the end helping those in society. The problem is today more than ever in American history this quest for profit in business is destroying our society. The rationality in business has been completely removed from business discourse. Today more than ever we need decisions to be made with a rational basis that looks out for those in society and provides the best possible outcomes for all people and not just those who own businesses.

Corporations carry the power to provide the goods and services we all need while providing people with employment that provides for people and their children. This is a tremendous responsibility and to make decisions solely based on profit is a gross misuse of this power. Decisions should consider profit as a basis but primarily focus on the full ramifications of their actions absent of the consideration of monetary benefit.

While corporations and industrialization have brought us the modern goods and services we receive they have also contributed too much turmoil within society in the modern era. One only has to look at the current situation in the United States and globally to see how the quest for profit absent of rationality has caused great unrest and turmoil for humans.

II.
In the United States we have millions of houses being foreclosed, children experiencing malnutrition and people generally losing hope in ever finding a job that can legitimately provide for their family. We have entire cities that are economically abandoned and impoverished. Millions of Americans lack health insurance and if they experience a life threatening injury they could be turned down by hospitals. These people turn for help and are turned away in many incidences because of the mentality in America that helping people is socialism which is concluded as somehow being evil. The worst part about this scenario is that it is not the fault of those who are unemployed and underpaid; they experience this suffering at the whim of those who make

business decisions based purely on personal profit. The owners and managers of business make these decisions but do not realize the consequences of their actions. They know they are firing someone but they do not understand that the macro-economic trend of firing employees for profit is eliminating the consumer base in the economy which is causing the recession.

On top of causing a recession millions of Americans are suffering in what was once known as a great nation. Even in some third world countries citizens are provided with free shelter, food and health care. In America our citizens are being wrongfully laid off and thrown on the street while we do nothing to help them because of the economic culture we have. It is immoral to say the least of how we treat the disadvantaged among us in our society.

The power base that is the ownership class of companies in the United States has been consistently lobbying government through the Republican Party. This lobbying has created a government and political culture that provides for needs and wants of business owners rather than the general populous of our nation. Barack Obama has been a president who has sought to represent the masses of citizens rather than only those who own and operate business. He has run into a huge backlash from the business owning and fundamentalist religious classes. This clash has ground any government action to a halt. In a time where masses of people are suffering as a result of the exploitation of business and current social trends there is hardly any help but a

gridlock in government over petty differences
in ideology.

Clashes between those in government who
believe helping others through government is
blasphemy against our beliefs and against
those who believe government is the basis to
which we can stop the suffering of our
citizens. The clash in ideology has made it
nearly impossible to get anything passed in
government to help people. Millions of
Americans are finding that they are unemployed
and either were denied unemployment benefits
or are running out of benefits. Millions of
Americans do not have access to basic health
care services while millions of children do
not have access to the proper nutrition and
clothing that they need. Businesses continue
to unjustly fire millions of Americans over
technicalities, and those who have run out of
unemployment benefits then become homeless.
This is all a result of the policies of the
business owning and religious fundamentalist
class which has geared our economic system to
filter wealth into their hands while
bankrupting those who work below them. After
bankrupting the masses of people they continue
to lobby government to stop government from
creating programs of which will help alleviate
the suffering of the masses of people. These
people continue to stop Barack Obama and the
government from implementing policies to help
the disadvantaged in society. They do this
because they do not fully understand the
ramifications of the economic ideology they
adhere to. They believe they are helping to
keep our nation prosperous because of the
embedded culture of neo-liberalism in
economics which is basically a hands-off

policy. They do not see the macro-economic effects of this policy and they also do not identify with those who suffer as they live in immense luxury. For them this system has worked because they have become extravagantly wealthy but, while they become wealthy the masses of people become desperate and poor. This causes them to stubbornly hang on to the ideology they have adhered to for decades and fight against the new government policies of Barack Obama and the left wing in America.

We as the United States have not been able to accomplish half of what we could to stop the suffering of our people and change our system to create fair growth in the future. Our government and national political debate accomplish nothing while our citizens continue to suffer. We face this road block in the ideology of individualism that is neither sustainable or a prosperous system in the future. We must get past this ideological milestone so that we can create economic and political policies that look out for all people and not just wealthy individuals.

III.

Currently the people who are suffering and held down in our current system feel a complete lack of hope or promise for the future. They lack the basic services and goods that they need at no fault of their own. Some people go from being a top contributor in a company to an unemployed desperate person over night. They are laid off with no thought of the ramifications of the action. The companies simply lay off a few workers and force the remaining workers to work harder than ever to make up for the workers lost. This way they only have to pay ten workers salaries and get the amount of work done that they could with fifteen or twenty. Meanwhile, the managers and owners get to pocket the money while the current workers work twice as hard, and the laid off workers lose their home and all they have worked for their entire lives. Then, these men and women attempt to lobby for help from government to keep their children in a home and fed and from this there becomes a huge backlash from the Republicans who say it is 'un-American' to provide help for these people; they simply think they should just find another job although this may not be as easy as they seem to think.

The problem with this is that every other company in our country is doing the exact thing as the one that just laid someone off unjustly. The person may be one of a thousand applicants and the one person that is chosen is going to have to complete the work that multiple workers did before and this of course is going to be at a lower wage and longer hours. This is the prospect that one of out of thousands of Americans may have if they are unemployed. All together upwards of forty million people in America are unemployed and many find themselves living off unemployment insurance, which is a small percentage of what they need to pay all of the bills that are inherent in our lives. Soon these people run out of unemployment benefits and are left with almost nothing to provide for their families while business owners and managers experience record profits as their labor costs shrink exponentially. This is how extreme individualism and success can cause harm to

our country and the world. The individual
business owners and managers seek to become as
wealthy as they can with their current status
and do not use rationality as a guiding force
in decisions because the bottom line is their
individual success and not the welfare of the
people around them. The drive for individual
success clouds the rationality in which people
make decisions. The more intense the
individualism, the more selfish and harmful
actions can become. If a person does not see
the harm in what they do they will continue to
repeat the behavior. If individualism is
celebrated and looked up to then of course
they will repeat it. The only problem is the
intense individualism and selfishness in
economics and politics has led us into our
current global economic crisis.

IV.

The way in which we organize ourselves in
society is centuries, if not thousands of
years old. Our modern technology has allowed
for a few people to produce many, many goods.
Previously one person would produce something
and either trade it with someone else's goods
or sell it for a monetary value. The invention
of money as a trade tool was developed under
this state in which individuals traded a
service or good that they produced
individually. This trade supported humans as
everyone had something they were good at
producing such as clothing or baskets and
food. Today we live in a much different world.
We do not have millions of people producing
the same thing and trading amongst their local
communities, instead we have a few people

operating large production centers that provide goods for nearly everyone on the planet. The way society produces goods and services has changed drastically since the social system of trade with monetary notes was implemented. With the huge change in how we run our economy and the technological advances that can eliminate suffering that previous generations endured, we have kept the same system and it has stifled the ability to make progress as a species. Instead of a system of equal trade among humans we have a system which filters wealth into the hands of those who own and control the mass production centers. They then selfishly organize the production centers to squeeze the most profit out of the business at the expense of the workers and the people who use their products.

At the same time humanity is able to produce more products and services that can help eliminate suffering and create a better world, and we also use the ability to do so as a method of coercion and a way of making individuals wealthy instead of using it as a tool for all humans. As our social organization lags thousands of years behind our technology and industrialization it causes the world to suffer needlessly. If we optimized the way society was organized under industrialization we could use our modern world to provide goods and services for everyone and not simply those who have ownership stakes in mass industry. Currently a lot of pain and suffering is caused from modern industrialization but it can be used for the betterment of all. We just have to organize ourselves properly and take advantage of the positives of industrialization and the modern world.

If we were to use the power of our modern industrial and technological infrastructure we could do many good things in the world, currently this is not the case. In some ways the mass industrial centers monopolize business and the ability to make money in one area and leave other cities destitute and broke. This mode of capitalism, which consists of companies expanding and conquering other corporations to become huge business monopolies, is not a sustainable system. It has contributed to the poverty of billions worldwide while making a few million incredibly wealthy. It has also contributed to military conflicts around the world. The expansion of companies around the world has given way to the use of governments and militaries to help expand the scope and reach of companies.

In early 19th century America the military was used in many conflicts that would set up business opportunities for American companies across the globe. This led to the deaths of many innocent people. It also resulted in near slave labor from many people who lived in the area. The aggressive expansion of companies around the world has not only contributed to job loss in America but it has led to inhumane working conditions for foreigners. Globalization which is an inherently good thing is being corrupted by the way in which it is implemented. Companies that were successful in employing Americans and selling their goods to Americans as well as others globally became obsessed with profit and

changed the way they did business to
experience more monetary gain at the expense
of American citizens. These companies
capitalized on the ability to get much cheaper
labor and to have evaded taxation. This has
not only led to unemployment among Americans
but also has led to a decrease in government
revenue to help build our nation. These trends
are both negative to our society and are
crippling our nation but at the same time are
making individuals that carry ownership in
these companies extravagantly wealthy.

There is an extreme disconnect between what
is good for individuals in a company and what
is good for all society. This is because our
system caters to individuals who want to
exploit wealth. Globalization of business for
profit is just one of the trends that has led
to unemployment and suffering. Globalization
in its idea is a noble and positive trend. It
is the motives and the way in which it is
implemented which has caused us problems
worldwide. Countries that hold American owned
businesses and production become limited by
copyright from making the businesses work for
the good of their people.

They are forced to abide by the will of
those in America who want to keep the labor
prices down and the workers docile and
accepting of their current situation.
Meanwhile Americans lose their careers and
become unemployed in a country where the
economic ideology does not allow for caring or
helping with their situation. This is a gross
misuse of the ability that comes with
industrialization and modern technology. We
have the ability to create a better world with

these advents but we focus on economic
competition and individuals becoming massively
wealthy while masses of people are either
stagnant or suffer. Individuals who happen to
be attached to ownership in industry can not
only live a life of luxury but use their
wealth as a tool of coercion to align the
world with their interests. Someone in this
situation does not have to feel the suffering
of others who are not in their position, and
also have no reason to look into their
suffering as they can surely entertain
themselves with almost limitless options. They
may own three houses and many cars and feel
that a bad day is not being able to book a
flight to their favorite vacation spot. A bad
day to the masses of people consists of losing
their job which they toil over and being
evicted while becoming homeless and starving.
When they ask for help they are either denied
because of American ideology or they are
looked at as lazy and inferior because of
their situation.

V.

   The actions taken by those who are
privileged in this world directly result in
the suffering of these people. The ideology
behind why they make these actions that harm
people is to blame. The idea that they are
successful and wealthy by their own individual
means is false. The only way one can become
extravagantly wealthy is with help of many
people providing labor and resources.

   The extravagant wealth is a result of
exploiting those who make the products or
perform the service that the owner sells. The
ideology that these people have works for

them, however, it does not work for society. It allows certain individuals to rise up, exploit and become very wealthy and powerful. Once wealthy and powerful they implement policies which will maintain their system and keep the masses of people below them weak and docile. This keeps them working and providing the ability for those in power to keep turning profit. This has created economic growth in the United States and around the world but it has done so in a very unbalanced fashion which could lead to catastrophe for the world economy. Centers of production become isolated in areas of which lead to the most profit for owners. This abandons other areas of the world and leads to unemployment which decreases the spending power of certain areas and further eliminates businesses' focus on the region. This is what is happening in the foreign business flight of American corporations, they abandon regions of America and leave most of the citizens unemployed.

They cannot spend on consumer goods so businesses further abandon the region and the area becomes destitute and broke. This foreign flight creates jobs in foreign areas for people of the region but it is at the lowest wage the company can get away with and with the most docile workers who will work for very long hours with little or no benefit. The globalization of the world economy is to be strived for but it should be executed in a fair and intelligent manner which will lead to sustainable growth.

This leads us back to the same quagmire that occurs in human society which is the elite in society versus the masses of people

who seek to live out a good life. The elite in
society attempt to shape the world view of
those in society to suit their individual
needs. In our case; in the modern world the
elite in society have retained so much power
that one action of policy they implement can
have far reaching effects that most would not
be able to fully fathom. In our modern world
an individual or group of business owners can
reside over thousands if not hundreds of
thousands of employees. Their products or
services may be the foundation onto which
millions of people live their lives on.

VI.

As you can see one leader of group of
leaders in these companies can affect millions
of people and in some cases billions. If they
base their decisions on a motive of personal
profit and it harms the people they serve it
can create devastating consequences to the
balance of things in the world. The scope of
people that they affect is huge and even
though they feel they are an isolated entity
they are not. They carry huge responsibility
and their actions carry great weight in human
society. The reckless decisions they make are
almost criminal in the amount of lives they
can affect negatively. At the whim of
corporate leaders thousands of families can be
thrown into poverty. Children lose their homes
and become desperate, hungry and cold from the
actions that some take in the name of American
economic ideology and profit. The elite in
companies continue to rake in profits and live
lavished lifestyles while the lives of the
masses of people exploited by them continue to
suffer. This system is not moral and it is

nearly criminal. It is a mass exploitation for the elite. The elite continue to release propaganda efforts to maintain the American ideology that has been put in place to keep these people in their current privileged position. The main focus of the ideology is making the masses of people maintain their blind work ethic and eventually they will become one of the wealthy ones. This of course is simply to keep the masses of people working for less pay while it continues to benefit the owners and managers of business. If this continues the wealth and power of those who own and control industry will only increase, while the ability for the masses of people to bargain for a better life, will become more and more unlikely. The more economic power that the wealthy and elite have the more they will be able to coerce people to work under their conditions. From their perspective if they make people desperate and divided they will be forced to comply with the one thing that will give them even a little money; when this happens the will of society will be even less heard and the personal profit of the elite and wealthy will decide the major decisions of the human race.

The decision making process of the elite and wealthy is the farthest thing from rational and it can have devastating effects to the balance of the world. Currently governmental decisions are being driven by investors and leaders of banks worldwide. Governments are looking out for the profit of these people. Instead of looking out for the people of their nation; countries are cutting social spending to put individual investors in a position that they will continue to enjoy the lavished profits they have had in the past. Countries around the world are making decisions based on the profit of individual wealthy elite over the good of all in society. The people in these countries are being cut off from government programs which allow them to have shelter, food and fair work. This is being done as a nod to banks and wealthy investors around the world so that they do not downgrade the "credit ratings" which is highly subjective to how the rating agency gains monetarily from a country. Countries are implementing austerity cuts to social welfare programs that keep the country afloat.

Elite in governments are being offered huge amounts of money to agree to the cuts to keep investors making profit. They are completely disconnected from the plight of the people in their nation. They are making decisions based on profit and they are not thinking rationally about what they are doing to their people. This has resulted in clashes between citizen protestors and elite in government and banking which seek to cut cost at the expense of the masses of people who are protesting. Countries around the world are experiencing mass protests and clashes with police who are paid by the elite. These protests have just started to rise up in the United States but are prevalent in many countries such as Spain, Greece, the United Kingdom and many countries in the Middle East and North Africa. These are cases in which the masses of people seek to take back the decision making processes for the people and to make rational decisions that work for everyone and not just those who have wealth and control industry.

The World in Our Hands

Adam M. Yeoman

Solutions for a Better World

*U*ltimately; we as humans hold the key to this planet and decide whether we suffer or prosper; the world is in our hands. We can change our world for the worse or the better. We have created much of the suffering that is inherent with our version of capitalism and money exchange. The system inherently gives control of society to elite who stand to profit off of the suffering of workers and lower class citizens. We have kept this system for many years and it has only contributed to more and more exploitation. This exploitation is coincided with the largest transfer of wealth from the masses of people to outrageously wealthy individuals in world history. This has caused mass unemployment, mass poverty and the loss of hope of millions. This system also has pinned elite in some countries against the elite in others over petty differences.

We are all humans and wish for the same for our planet but because of the elite control of nations, military conflicts have arose over the world in the last few hundred years that have created an essential hell on Earth for people affected by these conflicts. These conflicts and the poverty that people experience can be avoided. The human ability and spirit can solve huge problems. Currently this ability and spirit is sometimes channeled into the wrong areas such as building technological weapons of mass destruction and churning un-godly business profits while forcing thousands of employees out of work. With a cooperative effort channeled in the right direction humans could create a world where suffering is minimized and all people benefit from the world we share.

Currently this is not the case. Most of the good that comes from mass production and technology is filtering to wealthy people of the world while keeping wages and the lives of those workers who produce the products stagnant. Military conflicts are being taken by governments for less than moral reasons and have everything to do with wealth, power and the ideology that fits the former. This happens because the decision making process is limited to the elite and there is an ideological structure that is circulated through propaganda that keeps most people believing that they know what is best.

This is a dictatorship in disguise of a democracy. We are led to believe we carry the decision making process of our country but this is not the case. We vote for leaders who have already been chosen by elite to suit their needs. We do have a choice from two different parties but they are both already puppets of the current system before finishing their first year of office. The economic power holders in our society hold most of the power as they run under a dictatorship with owners and managers making decisions with no input from employees. This leads to lobbying from the ownership class to government and gives these people and their interests a majority of the political representation while the masses of people barely gain any real representation from our political system. The entire system ends up being rigged to provide for the lavished lifestyle of the elite while the masses of workers are kept inline through a robust legal system which is set up by the people who stand to gain from the strict stance on working individuals. This is clearly not a sustainable system for the masses of people who continue to suffer. Everything in the world is stacked against those who work for a living and do not have ownership stakes in industry. Anyone who does own industry can find their way out of many problems normal people would have had to face. If the wealth that elite gained did not have such an adverse affect on the masses of people, no one would care that they have become massively wealthy while we are just satisfied with our situation. The reason something must be done is the irrationality that the wealthy in businesses display is the direct cause of suffering for the masses of people. Children are starving and cold because wealthy men and women cannot live without two yachts instead of one.

II.

It is time for a change. It is time that
the masses of people rise up and form their
own representation as it is clearly lacking in
the common political realm. On Earth we should
have the ability to provide for our families
with shelter, food and clothing. These things
should not be infringed on. It does not matter
if there is money involved or not. These
things should be natural human rights. The
first step in creating a better world is
giving the people who need it the essentials
in surviving whether they work for it or not.
The changes we can make are changes in which
will give the common people a voice in
economic and political decisions. We need to
have a true democracy. Currently our country
is driven by elite in government, media, and
economics instead of the people of our nation.
This causes the irrational behavior that leads
to the suffering of our people. We must seek
to implement real democracy in our country and
give suffering people a real voice in the
national political and economic debate. This
can come as a movement of the people or as a
nod to progress by the elite to allow for
democratic voices to be heard in our economy
and government. To begin to fix the problems
we face we must start to look at the bigger
picture of our economy and how individual
selfish actions in one economic sector can
have far reaching effects. Our nation was
founded on democratic principles but has
turned into more of a corporate oligarchy. We
must take into account the issues that
everyone faces and not just those with money
to buy representation.

The system of individualism and wealth in elite hands is not sustainable and must be altered. If we as a species just cooperate we could accomplish so many great things especially with the level of technology we have achieved. Currently; we are bound by the rules of capitalism and the interests of wealthy people who wish to keep their industries at the top. This halts economic and technological growth while leaving people unemployed and suffering.

III.

If we put forth a cooperative effort to create jobs and industries that seek to provide for humans and stem suffering we could accomplish it together. We cannot accomplish this now because of the imbedded capitalist system. Capitalism was designed as an engine for economic growth but has become a hindrance to growth and prosperity. In fact the selfishness that is displayed under capitalism has bankrupted the world economy and has left millions unemployed and suffering. It has ignored starving regions of the world because it is not profitable to feed starving people. We have ignored genocide and mass starvation at an alarming rate in the last few centuries but when it comes to helping out business leaders we can accomplish just about anything. Capitalism and industrialization were invented as a tool to provide for humanity, yet it has been hijacked to circulate wealth into the top percent of society's hands. Fair competition and the elimination of monopolies keep businesses acting somewhat fairly but we have experienced the largest conglomeration of businesses in our history. One conglomeration controls entire industries and there is no real competition. These monopolies lobby government and draw up the law code so that they continue to be the monopolies and draw massive profits.

This has turned capitalism into a destructive force rather than a helpful one. The initial good that was caused by ingenuity, creativity and entrepreneurship has been replaced with a dictatorship by massive monopolies which seek to keep progress limited to what will continue to profit them. Essentially we live under a system in which monopolies seek to control society so that it will continue to benefit them and only them. There are huge conflicts of interest with this system. The monopolies of companies and companies in general are not concerned with providing employment for humans. They are concerned only with making a profit through business ventures. There is no moral or ethical concern to them. This is why they display no moral or ethical concern when dealing with employees or the world. This system is led by dictators who seek to drive productivity and production to suit the profits they would like to see. There is no input from employees or the people of the nation they operate in. This clearly is not democratic nor is it a healthy system for the good of all in our country or the world. The squeeze for profits at the expense of workers and consumers leads to irrational decisions that are not the best for humanity.

To correct many of the modern problems we have we must institute democracy into the economic sector. This is not government mandated communism but simply democracy, where the people of the world have a say in what their company does to their employees and what direction their company should take as an organization. The profit margin that companies experience should be nearly equally distributed to the employees of the company with maybe a little extra going to those who founded the company but not all of the profits. This would take away the blind irrationality that comes with running a company solely for making extravagant profit. This would be replaced by rationality from a democratic voice from the people of the organization and the greater voice of all people in the world. This is just one trend that would eliminate a lot of the irrationality that is causing people suffering and stunting economic growth and prosperity on earth. Another form of democracy that can help gear economics and people's lives in general is the use of government which previously has been designed to suit only the elite.

We need a new form of progressive government that provides equal representation to all people and not just those who have access to lobbyists and able to give high priced donations. The government is supposed to be a representation of all people and a voice for the common good of society. It has been hijacked by the capitalist system of wealthy elite who gain influence by exploiting workers for wealth and then using their wealth to get policies implemented that suit them in government. The government has become a crony for these people and not for the good of all Americans. When real democracy takes place in our government and among our corporations a rational voice will be heard. Rational decisions that suit all Americans will be made. It is obvious that irrationality of our government and in our corporations is due to special interests of wealthy elite who profit from the policies and actions. The question is how can we take our country back for all people without starting violent conflict or causing mass unrest?

IV.

The biggest thing we can do is to get the ideas and concepts out to the masses of people so that they understand exactly why we are in this situation. Many in our country have been indoctrinated with political and economic philosophy that has been provided by the elite and wealthy to keep the status quo. We must take down these ideas with rational debate of what is really happening in our society. There is a built-in effect in our society that when someone challenges how our economy and political structure is run can have wide reaching affects on all of society.

The quest for endless profits is the direct reason for the maltreatment of labor and the citizens of country. I am not advocating we all be exactly the same and no one should be rewarded for hard work, this is just what the elite and wealthy will tell you that people like me want. I simply want to stop the exploitation of masses of people and keep a fair and just society so that we "ALL" can prosper in the future. In order for us to prosper in the future and provide the essentials of life we must turn away from the blind individualism that leads to extraordinary wealthy individuals controlling industry for their own profit while leaving most of the world unemployed. This blind individualism is not sustainable nor is it even healthy to begin with. The greatest ability we as humans have is to cooperate and use our ingenuity, creativity and work to shape our reality on earth. Currently we are using this in a selfish fashion that provides wealth for few people while leaving untapped the potential of millions of people who could contribute greatly to society. This has to do with the complete hands of policy of our economic ideology. The economy should be a representation of the people in society just as the government is. The thing about modern industrialization is that it allows for individuals to carry mass control over other portions of society and not do so politically but economically.

The theories of privatization essentially give these people unchecked power. The government is hard-pressed to intervene while members of the company are threatened with loss of employment if they say anything against the company's current structure. It allows for dictatorship driven industry to make the important decisions that affect many people on this earth. This is the negative of our type of capitalism. Dictators of industry make irrational decisions based purely on profit which carry wide reaching negative effects on society. The problem with the current economic theory is obvious. Individuals become wealthy and subordinate the working population. On the other hand communism does not allow for the proper distribution of production centers and variety in production. It can make economic growth stagnant. The negatives of communism are a lack of consumer goods and stagnant economic progress. The issue with capitalism is the intense greed and irrationality that leaves many people of the world without hope or purpose while others profit off of others' misery. I am suggesting a hybrid between the ideals of entrepreneurship, creativity and ingenuity and that of perfect social organization in communism. We have perfected the ability to run business in varying locations and successfully produce goods. This is what we do in good in America. What we are horrible at is organizing our society in a balanced way which maximizes our potential. Currently, we live in a rat race where the winners get to the top and then organize society so they stay there. They then spit on everyone below them who lost. This is immoral and should not be tolerated in our modern world but is because of the ideology inherent in capitalism. A system which uses both the good of capitalism, the ability to mass produce goods, and the democratic organization of a healthy society that comes with communism; is ideal.

To solve the economic issues in America and the world we need to institute democratic principles among the corporations of the world. Rationality needs to replace the quest for endless profits. Any given company in the world right now could take capital from the tremendous profits they experience and hire more employees, reinvest in the company and increase the wage of current employees. This would be the rational choice giving the current global scenario but this would of course eats at the profits of extremely wealthy individuals. If they did do this in a rational matter instantly the current employees would have more purchasing power and spend more on consumer goods. The newly hired employees would also instantly circulate money back into the economy.

V.

   The circular effect that results in capitalism when people spend money would bring our economy back to life as people would now have money to spend. The money spent would reach corporations who would use it to grow and create more jobs while providing better jobs as well as better service to customers. If every business used their profits to reinvest in the company and the employees in just one quarter of the business cycle it would have a tremendous impact on the current global recession. This is the opposite of selfish and it is of course rational. These types of rational moves in the economy could help stop many of the problems we as humans face. The biggest problem we have in the industrialized world is the selfishness and irrationality of economics. If anything, the advent of industrialization requires that we as humans become overly intelligent in the manner in which we use the powers of industrialization and technology as a tool to help humanity rather than harm it. The hurdles we face with this problem have to do with the systematic propaganda that has been released by elite and wealthy which has convinced people that it is actually unmoral to have a say in business. When it is the opposite in reality; man can control thousands of others' lives if not millions because of the advent of

industrialization and these men or women have
a responsibility to the people who they can
affect. It is intensely immoral that these
people make actions in which affect millions
that are based on a selfish desire for profit
rather than caring and rationality.

VI.

To correct these problems there must be a
common voice debunking the misinformation that
has perpetuated actions that harm many people.
Raising awareness of the importance of gearing
business for the common good and instituting
real democracy in government and business
would help change the minds of many people and
therefore change the actions they make and the
general balance of the world. Once rationality
and the adherence to the common good are
established in business and politics things
can begin to correct themselves and make
actions which are in line with the common good
of humans. To understand the reasons why
things are the way they are gives tremendous
power in knowing how to solve the large
problems. The main reason for the current
global economic climate is the selfishness in
economics which creates wealth for some and
mass labor for many. This can be fixed with
democracy and rationality in economics along
with a cooperative effort by humans to shape
the world we live in. This does not mean that
humans are going to turn into lazy hippies as
described by American right wing media, it
means that we as humans can use our combined
power on earth to make a better world and
shape it for a sustainable and healthy future
for all humans to come after us.

Instituting rationality and cooperation in economics and politics will start by changing minds. It will then result in rational actions by us as humans to solve the issues we face in a cooperative manner. Surely a future in which all humans can cooperate for the good of all on earth can accomplish things beyond our current imagination.

Bibliography

De, Blij Harm J., and Alexander B. Murphy. Human
Geography: Culture, Society,and Space. New York
; Toronto: J. Wiley, 1999

Janda, Kenneth, Jeffrey M. Berry, and Jerry Goldman.
The   Challenge of Democracy: Government in
America. Boston: Houghton Mifflin, 1992

Locke, John. The Second Treatise of Government.
Indianapolis: Hackett, 1690.

Loewen, James W. Lies My Teacher Told Me: Everything
Your American History Textbook Got Wrong. New York:
Simon & Schuster, 2007. Print.

Marx, Karl, Friedrich Engels, and E. J. Hobsbawm.
The Communist Manifesto: a Modern Edition. London:
Verso, 1998. Print.

Plato, and Benjamin Jowett. Plato: the Republic.
Norwalk, CT: Easton, 1980.

Ravenhill, John. Global Political Economy. Oxford:
Oxford UP, 2008.

Rousseau, Jean-Jacques. The Social Contract. New
York: Penguin, 2006. Print

Strauss, Leo, and Joseph Cropsey. History of
Political Philosophy. Chicago: University of
Chicago, 1987.

T. Web. 08 Oct. 2011. <http://rt.com/>.

ABOUT THE AUTHOR

Adam M. Yeoman is a Rochester, NY native with a Bachelor's Degree in Political Science and International Studies (May, 2011). After being homeschooled in high school, he obtained his Associates Degree from Genesee Community College in Batavia NY where he also played for the college's basketball team, and then went on to get his Bachelor's at the State University of New York at Brockport, while also playing semi-professional basketball. While this is his first book, he has written various news articles for examiner.com. Facing the possibility of attending the London School of Politics and Economics, he decided on beginning his book instead as a result of his great passion to effect the world. He hopes that this book will help him to influence the world especially during a time of global economic crisis. With the help of his girlfriend, the book was written, edited, formatted and website also created all in a short 6 months.

Read more at www.theworldinourhands.yolasite.com

www.ingramcontent.com/pod-product-compliance
Lightning Source LLC
Chambersburg PA
CBHW031323290526
45784CB00014B/838